The Best Bread Machine Cookbook Ever

Ethnic Breads

Madge Rosenberg

A John Boswell Associates/King Hill Productions Book

HarperCollins*Publishers*

ACKNOWLEDGMENTS

To my parents, Esther and Jules Greenspan, for their faith in me.

Thanks to my husband, Barry, for the time and love he has given me. And thanks especially to Natalie Andersen, my sister, who set the standards as well as the pace and tested every loaf.

FIRST EDITION

Design: Barbara Cohen Aronica
Index: Maro Riofrancos

Library of Congress Cataloging-in-Publication Data

Rosenberg, Madge.
    The best bread machine cookbook ever.   Ethnic breads / Madge
Rosenberg.—1st ed.
        p.   cm.
    "A John Boswell Associates/King Hill Productions Book."
    Includes bibliographical references (p.   ) and index.
    ISBN 0-06-017093-X
    1. Bread.   2. Automatic bread machines.   3. Cookery,
International.   I. Title.
TX760.R83   1994
641.8'15—dc20   93-50765

94 95 96 97 98 HC 10 9 8 7 6 5 4 3 2 1

Contents

Russia, Hungary, and Poland are among the countries that have given us familiar ethnic loaves: rye, pumpernickel, babka, black bread, bialies, and more.

From the sunny countries surrounding the Mediterranean come irresistible recipes for savory breads—Tapenade Bread, Greek Oregano and Lemon Bread—sweet breads—Tiramisu, Savarin—and for the best-ever bread machine Brioche.

Introduction

Welcome to the Breads of the World

With a bread machine, making loaf after loaf of aromatic freshly baked bread that is crisp outside and moist and full of flavor inside soon becomes as easy as it is exciting. With this volume, you and your bread machine are ready for adventures, for breads from cultures as far away as East Africa, as seductive as the South of France. Flat breads, sweet breads, sturdy ryes, pumpernickels, feathery almond breads, and coconut loaves are just a few.

Many of the breads in the book are finished completely in the bread machine; many others use the dough cycle for the sticky, laborious kneading, and leave the fun part of design and shaping to you. These formed breads are then left to rise and are baked in a conventional oven. Your creativity will come out as you become comfortable with your bread machine. Here are recipes for hors d'oeuvres and dessert breads, a plan for a Chinese *dim sum* party from your bread machine, for sandwich breads or doughnuts for children, for holiday gift breads, and for picture-perfect classics, like brioche and pita.

Enjoying Swiss Peasant Bread, Bermuda Fruitcake, and Indian Naan makes you more than an armchair traveler: it lets you dip a little deeper into life-styles so different from ours, yet with bread in common. If a picture is worth a thousand words, how would you value fragrance and flavor? The richness of Christmas Bread in even the poorest Greek villages or the elaborate sign of the cross on Ethiopian flat bread tell us how important religion is in these cultures.

Cardamom and toasted almonds give us a scent of Scandinavia, cumin and onions of Latin America, garlic of the Mediterranean. These magic carpet breads will transport you to far-off lands.

If you love to travel and want to bring back memories, or if you are not a traveler but a curious baker and adventurous eater, this book will tell you how to make breads from faraway places. Some of these recipes are little known in these parts; others, like Danish and Kaiser Rolls and Cuban Bread, express our melting-pot culture. The bread machine and this book will speed you on your exploration of the breads of the world.

About the Bread Machines

Millions of bread machines have been sold in the United States. New brands continue to arrive, and new models appeared during the writing of this book. Not all brands are sold throughout the entire country, and a few use different brand names in different markets. We did not find any losers. Every machine we used made good bread. Some machines make crustier bread than others, usually requiring at least a four-hour cycle. The breads made on a shorter cycle have less contrast between crust and interior. We rarely used the special "whole wheat" or "French bread" cycles, because we had such good results with the basic bread and dough cycles on each machine. All of the machines have delayed timing so that you can add the ingredients at one time and the machine will knead and bake the bread up to thirteen hours later, which allows you to set up your bread maker at night and wake up in the morning to fresh bread.

DAK
These machines are available through the DAK Industries catalog, out of California, which has an 800 number. The less expensive model makes a 1-pound loaf in four hours. It has a domed glass on top of a round body. The new Turbo

Baker II looks the same, but makes and bakes a 1½-pound loaf in two and a half hours.

HITACHI

The Hitachi is the only machine we tried that lets you make a ½-pound, 1-pound, 1½-pound, or 2-pound loaf in the same machine. It will also make jam and steam rice, and newer models have a rapid cycle of just over two hours. The basic cycle made very crusty loaves.

MAXIM

The Maxim model BB I makes a 1½-pound bread in two hours and twenty minutes. At this setting, it makes whole wheat and rye breads, too, that are good but not crusty. For crusty breads, stop at the end of the first kneading and rising, and begin the bread cycle again. The extra kneading and rising will make an even better bread.

PANASONIC, OR NATIONAL

Panasonic model BT65P made very crusty 1½-pound loaves. There are five cycles on the machine, from a two-hour quick bread cycle to a seven-hour crisp bread cycle. Even the dough cycle is over two hours. The basic bread cycle made such good, crusty loaves that the seven-hour cycle was not necessary. There is a separate yeast dispenser, but no beeper to indicate the addition of raisins or nuts. This is the only machine that makes a traditional, horizontal loaf.

REGAL

The removable crumb tray makes this one of the easiest machines to keep clean. It also has indicators that tell you what stage you are at in the process: kneading, rising, baking. The raisin bread cycle, which has a beeper signal for adding ingredients, and the basic bread cycle each take three hours and forty minutes including a twenty-minute cool down. The rapid cycle is just under two hours. The Regal makes a 1-pound loaf.

SANYO

The Sanyo Bread Factory Plus makes a 1-pound loaf of whole wheat, French, sweet, or basic bread on cycles from three to four hours. There is both a rapid and a regular whole wheat cycle. The distribution of added raisins or nuts is especially even in the Bread Factory. As a special safety feature, this machine stops when the lid is raised. The viewing glass in the top is just large enough to let you see what is happening inside.

TRILIUM BREADMAN

The Trilium Breadman is easy to clean and simple to use. It features a buzzer for adding ingredients, a small window at the top, a three-year warranty, and an instruction video.

WELBILT

The Welbilt is my original bread machine; it has made over two hundred breads and is still going strong. This is one of the originals with a basic bread cycle and a dough cycle, but even the dough cycle has a beeper for adding ingredients. This rectangular model makes a 1-pound loaf in two hours and twenty minutes. The big, round Welbilt has a domed glass top and makes a 1½-pound bread in four hours.

WESTBEND

The same machine will make a 1- or 1½-pound loaf on a three-hour rapid yeast cycle or a regular three-hour and forty-minute cycle. It has a three-hour "warmer" cycle that keeps the bread moist once it is baked. The machine comes with an instructional video and is made in the United States.

ZOJIRUSHI

We used the large machine that produces an almost 8-inch-high loaf in four hours. There is a glass top for viewing and a crumb tray for easy cleanup. In addition to a "Homemade Menu" you can program yourself, there are raisin, French bread, quick bread, dough, cake, and jam cycles. It gives you a great deal of flexibility and produces a tall, narrow loaf.

More machines are on the way from Black & Decker, Betty Crocker, and Toastmaster.

About the Ingredients

ACTIVE DRY YEAST

Yeast is made of tiny plants that change food—especially gluten and sugar—into carbon dioxide, which causes the bread to rise. Keep active dry yeast in the refrigerator. The machines are not timed for instant yeast or for fresh cake yeast, so use only *active dry yeast*.

BARLEY MALT SYRUP

This is extracted by sprouting and drying barley, which is a grain, and caramelizing its sugar. It adds a rich, barely sweet taste, while encouraging the yeast and sourdough to rise and produce richer, moister bread. It is available in health food stores.

CARAMEL COLORING

Most really dark breads are colored with burned sugar or caramel syrup. It sweetens the bread only slightly, but adds moisture as well as color. Making your own will ruin a pot and possibly your kitchen. A good mail-order source is listed on page 10.

COCONUT

Some recipes in this book call for flaked coconut. This is the ordinary shredded coconut found in packages in supermarkets. If your market sells grated fresh coconut in the produce section, by all means use that.

COCONUT MILK

Coconut milk is made by soaking grated fresh coconut meat in water, straining out the coconut, and saving the liquid, or "milk." Canned unsweetened coconut milk, found in the Thai or Asian foods sections of most supermarkets and in Asian markets, is a fine substitute. Do not use coconut cream, which is very sweet and is meant for drinks.

EGGS

Eggs add flavor and lightness and a golden color to bread. Egg substitutes can be used in any of these breads.

FATS

Oils, butter, margarine, lard, chicken fat, and solid vegetable shortening are all fats that make bread softer and tastier and preserve it longer. When oil is called for, unless olive oil is specified, use a flavorless polyunsaturated vegetable oil, such as safflower, canola, corn, or a mixed vegetable oil.

SALT

Salt not only adds flavor, it governs the power of the yeast. Salt slows down the yeast action; too much salt can kill the yeast. Too little salt lets the dough rise so fast that it may fall before it finishes baking. Salt is also a preservative, which keeps the bread from getting stale as quickly. Without salt, bread has a coarser quality because of the overly fast rising.

SOURDOUGH STARTER

This is an ingredient to keep on hand so you can make sourdough bread anytime: Mix 1 cup of flour with 1 cup of water and a pinch of yeast. Stir until creamy. Leave the mixture alone for a week in a large glass or plastic container, unrefrigerated. It is a living culture that bubbles and smells strange. The different strains of yeast in the atmosphere work on it. Sours made from the same ingredients vary from place to place because of the ambient conditions. No one has made San Francisco sourdough in the Midwest yet, although commercial bakeries have tried.

At least once a week, use your starter or discard ½ cup of it, and be sure to replenish it with equal amounts of flour and water stirred together until they are smooth and creamy. This keeps the starter fresh and active. After the initial week, you can store the starter in the refrigerator, but bring it up to room temperature for baking by making the water in the recipe just warmer than body temperature and mixing the two together before they go into the bread machine.

SWEETENERS

Sugar, brown sugar, honey, molasses, and fruits add sweetness and help brown the crust. The riper the fruit, the more sweetness it adds. Dried fruit adds concentrated sweetness.

WHEAT

Bread flour is made from high-gluten, or hard wheat without its germ or bran, but containing all the gluten from the grain. It rises better than any other flour.

Whole wheat flour has the bran and the germ but a lower proportion of gluten. It rises, but not as well as bread flour. Buy whole wheat bread flour, not pastry flour and choose the coarsest grind you can find; it is sometimes called graham flour.

Wheat bran is the outside of the wheat kernel. It contains much of the vitamins and most of the fiber.

Wheat germ is the center of the wheat kernel and it contains many nutrients and oils. Once a jar of wheat germ is opened, it should be refrigerated. Because of the high concentration of oil, it can go rancid quickly at room temperature.

Semolina is a wheat usually used for pasta. Made from durum wheat, it is strong and rises well.

Cracked wheat is the whole wheat kernel crushed into very small pieces but still coarser than the coarsest whole wheat flour. Some people soak it for an hour before using; I prefer not to because I like the crunch.

Bulgur is parboiled, dried, and cracked wheat kernels.

OTHER FLOURS AND GRAINS

Amaranth is a nutty, high-protein grain from Central America. Since it is very low in gluten, use small quantities along with a large amount of wheat flour. It has a bland flavor.

Cornmeal adds its own slightly sweet flavor, crumbly texture, and sunny color to bread if you use yellow cornmeal, as we did. Stone-ground meal is more distinctive, but the supermarket variety will serve.

Oats are just regular, old-fashioned oatmeal or, specifically, rolled oats. The same oats you use for breakfast cereal add their flavor and fiber to bread. All the oat bran is still there. Toast oats lightly in a 350 degree oven for 5 minutes to intensify their flavor.

Quinoa is a nutritious pearly grain from Peru, recently brought into the United States and popularized because of its high protein and mineral content.

Rye flour is high in protein, but low in gluten. Consequently, it will not rise on its own. From 20 to 30 percent of the flour content in a bread can be rye, but the rest needs to be high-gluten wheat flour, or you will have very heavy bread. White rye flour is used in "rye bread"; dark rye is used for "pumpernickel."

Source of Supplies

BARLEY MALT SYRUP AND
CARAMEL COLORING
Niblack Foods, Inc.
900 Jefferson Road, Bldng #5
Rochester, NY 14623
(716) 292-0790

CARAMEL COLORING
Mister Spiceman
169-06 Crocheron Avenue
Auburndale, NY 11358
(718) 358-5020

FLOURS AND GRAINS
Arrowhead Mills
110 So. Lawton
Hereford, TX 79045
(806) 364-0730

Deer Valley Farm
Box 173
Guilford, NY 13780-0173
(607) 764-8556

Elams
2625 Gardner Road
Broadview, IL 60153
(708) 865-1612

King Arthur Flour
RR 2 Box 56
Norwich, VT 05055
(800) 827-6836

Walnut Acres
Penns Creek, PA 17862
(800) 433-3998

Measuring

Read your owner's manual, because bread machines differ. Ingredients are put in in different orders, temperature requirements for the liquids differ, and minimum and maximum amounts of bread flour differ. In using any recipe in this book, be sure to follow the manufacturer's instructions. For best results, measure ingredients precisely. Too much liquid results in soggy, sunken bread. Too much flour makes bread heavy, coarse, and dry.

DRY INGREDIENTS
Measure over a plate or paper towel. Spoon flours, granulated sugar, and grains into a measuring cup until overflowing. Do not press down. Level by sweeping the excess off with an unserrated knife or spatula.

BROWN SUGAR AND BUTTER OR MARGARINE
Press firmly into a dry measuring cup or spoon. Level off the excess with an unserrated knife or spatula. If using brown sugar, sprinkle it into the flour; do not add in a single lump.

LIQUIDS
Use a standard liquid measuring cup and spoons. Check measurement at eye level.

STICKY INGREDIENTS (HONEY, MOLASSES, AND SO ON)
Oil cup or spoon first so that the sticky stuff will slide out easily. If the recipe calls for butter or oil, measure it first and the sticky ingredient second so you won't have to wash the measure in between.

Freezing

To freeze baked bread, let the loaf cool completely. Wrap the whole unsliced bread in plastic wrap, foil, or freezer paper, forcing out as much air as possible. To defrost, leave the bread wrapped at room temperature for two hours or overnight. Unwrap for another hour so that it will not be soggy. For quicker thawing, slice the bread before freezing.

To warm defrosted bread, place it in a preheated 300 degree oven for 15 to 20 minutes or microwave according to the oven manufacturer's instructions.

It is better to bake bread before freezing it. But if you want to freeze unbaked dough that has completed the dough cycle in the bread machine, brush it lightly with oil, wrap it well, and freeze. Keep the dough frozen for no more than two days, or it will lose its ability to rise. Richer doughs containing butter and sugar freeze best. To defrost, unwrap, cover loosely, and defrost overnight in the refrigerator. When defrosted, leave at room temperature in a draftfree place to rise. Do not leave dough unrefrigerated while defrosting, or the outside will begin to rise before the inside defrosts.

Helpful Hints

1. Before you slice or juice an orange or a lemon, peel off the zest, the colored part of the skin, with a swivel-bladed vegetable peeler. Save it for the many recipes that call for orange and lemon zest, candied or plain.

2. Before using nuts and seeds, toast them lightly in a 350 degree oven for about 5 minutes to bring out the flavor and then let cool.

3. Keep a piece of bread in an opened box of brown sugar. The sugar will stay soft; the bread will get hard.

4. When you remove baked bread from the machine, keep the loaf inverted until it is just cool enough to handle; then check to be sure the kneading blade has not remained in the loaf. If it has, remove it before turning the bread right side up. If you slice the bread with the blade still in it you will scrape the blade and remove some of the nonstick coating.

5. If your machine has a clear domed top and your bread is not browning, cover the top of the machine with aluminum foil to help the bread brown.

6. To store bread, place it in a plastic bag with a rib of celery to keep it fresher. Seal and store in a cool dry place. I find bread gets soggy in the refrigerator.

Common Problems and Their Solutions

PROBLEM	CAUSE	SOLUTION
1. Sunken top	Bread falls because dough is too wet	Reduce liquid by 1 tablespoon or add 2 tablespoons of flour.
2. Knotty, uneven top	Not enough moisture	Add 1 tablespoon of liquid or reduce flour by 2 tablespoons.
3. Mushroom top	Bread rises too fast and collapses	Reduce yeast by ¼ teaspoon.
4. Slices unevenly	Bread is too hot	Let bread cool before slicing.
5. Top is raw	Too much dough	Reduce size of recipe by 10 to 20 percent.
6. Pocket of sticky dough in sweet breads	Too much sugar or too little yeast	Add ¼ teaspoon yeast or reduce the sugar by 1 tablespoon.

Chapter One
Breads of Eastern Europe

Many of these recipes make the quintessential ethnic breads that we enjoy at local bakeries; dense, hearty, and chewy. The large Slovak, Polish, and Russian-Jewish immigration to the United States brought with it the babka, bagels, bialies, black bread, raisin pumpernickel, and kugelhopf, which are now so much a part of traditional American baking.

From Austria to Poland, Hungary, Romania, and the former Soviet Union and Czechoslovakia, bread is synonymous with food. If there is no bread, people are hungry, even if they have fruits and vegetables and milk. There is bread at every meal, on every picnic, at every party.

In Eastern Europe, spices are meager, imported, and costly. Instead loaves are often flavored with "sours," which come from a simple mixture of flour and water or from potatoes or onions. Caraway and poppy seeds dress up these rustic breads. If eggs or butter are added, it is because there is a holiday or a wedding celebration. It is the simplicity of these breads, along with their earthy taste and satisfying texture, that makes them so immensely appealing.

Russian Black Bread

Slightly sour, dense, and dark—what better bread for smoked turkey or ham, cold roast beef with grainy mustard, or with cream cheese sprinkled with chives and radish slices. A thick buttered slice is perfect with borscht.

SMALL LOAF (1 POUND)	INGREDIENTS	LARGE LOAF (1½ POUNDS)
1 teaspoon	active dry yeast	1½ teaspoons
1¾ cups	bread flour	2⅔ cups
½ cup	rye flour	¾ cup
1 teaspoon	salt	1½ teaspoons
½ cup	mashed potatoes	¾ cup
1 tablespoon	vegetable oil	1½ tablespoons
2 tablespoons	caramel coloring*	3 tablespoons
½ cup	sourdough starter**	¾ cup
½ cup	water	¾ cup

Add all ingredients in the order suggested by your bread machine manual and process on the bread cycle according to the manufacturer's directions.

*See mail-order sources on page 10. The caramel coloring can be omitted, but the bread will not be black; the flavor will be the same.

**After measuring out what is needed for this recipe, be sure to replenish your sourdough starter with equal amounts of flour and water.

Buckwheat Bread

Buckwheat blini, caviar, and vodka are the classic Russian culinary triangle. Substitute thin slices of buckwheat bread for the blini for an easy, sophisticated first course. If you toast the slices, brush them with melted butter just before serving. Golden caviar and salmon roe are good economical substitutes for imported beluga or sevruga. Small dishes of sour cream, finely chopped hard-cooked egg yolks and egg whites, and minced onion are part of the traditional presentation. For a festive New Year's Eve celebration, switch to Champagne instead of vodka.

SMALL LOAF (1 POUND)	INGREDIENTS	LARGE LOAF (1½ POUNDS)
1½ teaspoons	active dry yeast	2¼ teaspoons
1¾ cups	bread flour	2⅔ cups
½ cup	buckwheat flour	¾ cup
½ teaspoon	salt	¾ teaspoon
1 tablespoon	sugar	1½ tablespoons
1	whole egg	1
0	egg yolk	1
3 tablespoons	sour cream	¼ cup
3 tablespoons	vegetable oil	¼ cup
½ cup	water	¾ cup

Add all ingredients in the order suggested by your bread machine manual and process on the bread cycle according to the manufacturer's directions.

Raisin Pumpernickel

One of the greatest foods immigrating Jews brought to the United States from Eastern Europe is raisin pumpernickel—a sweet bread, so heavy with raisins that the dough barely holds them together. Our friend Flaherty always serves it with scallion-studded cream cheese and a good red wine. Or butter it lightly and have it with coffee any time of day.

SMALL LOAF (1 POUND)	INGREDIENTS	LARGE LOAF (1½ POUNDS)
1½ teaspoons	active dry yeast	2½ teaspoons
1¼ cups	bread flour	1¾ cups plus 2 tablespoons
⅔ cup	rye flour	1 cup
1 teaspoon	caraway seeds	1½ teaspoons
½ teaspoon	salt	¾ teaspoon
1 tablespoon	caramel coloring	1½ tablespoons
1 tablespoon	vegetable oil	1½ tablespoons
½ cup	sourdough starter*	⅔ cup
⅔ cup	water	1 cup
2 cups	raisins	3 cups

1. Add all ingredients except the raisins in the order suggested by your bread machine manual and process on the bread cycle according to the manufacturer's directions.

2. At the beeper (or at the end of the first kneading in the Panasonic, Sanyo, and National), add the raisins. Let cool completely before slicing.

*After measuring out what is needed for this recipe, be sure to replenish your sourdough starter with equal amounts of flour and water.

Baltic Bacon Bread

Traditionally, this recipe is made into buns, but I've found the flavors make a wonderful loaf. Wrap it in a towel and take it on a sunrise picnic, or make a lettuce and tomato sandwich for lunch.

SMALL LOAF (1 POUND)	INGREDIENTS	LARGE LOAF (1½ POUNDS)
¼ pound	bacon	⅓ pound
¼ cup	chopped onion	⅓ cup
1¼ teaspoons	active dry yeast	2 teaspoons
2 cups	bread flour	3 cups
2 tablespoons	powdered milk	3 tablespoons
½ teaspoon	salt	¾ teaspoon
1 tablespoon	sugar	1½ tablespoons
1	whole egg	1
0	egg white	1
⅔ cup	water	1 cup

1. Cook the bacon in a medium skillet over medium heat until very crisp. Drain on paper towels, leaving 1 teaspoon of rendered bacon fat in the pan. Cook the onion in the fat over medium heat until golden, about 5 minutes. Let cool.

2. Add all ingredients, including the bacon and onion, in the order suggested by your bread machine manual and process on the bread cycle according to the manufacturer's directions.

Georgian Cheese Bread
(Khachapuri)

This bread comes from the Georgian Republic, from its days as a rich dairy land, long before the Soviet Union existed. The dough encloses subtly spiced cheese enriched with butter and egg. Wrap this loaf in a tea towel and take it on a picnic. Or offer a wedge as a first course. With a hearty soup, it makes a satisfying meal.

Yield: 1 (10-inch) round loaf, enough for 10 as a first course

---

DOUGH

---

2 teaspoons	active dry yeast
2 cups	bread flour
1 tablespoon	sugar
1 teaspoon	salt
2 tablespoons	unsalted butter
¾ cup plus 2 tablespoons	water

FILLING

---

1 pound	Muenster cheese, shredded
1 tablespoon	unsalted butter
1	egg
1 tablespoon	ground coriander

1. Add all ingredients for the dough in the order suggested by your bread machine manual and process on the dough cycle according to the manufacturer's directions.
2. Mix together all the ingredients for the filling, cover, and refrigerate.
3. At the end of the dough cycle, remove the dough from the machine. Preheat the oven to 350 degrees.
4. On a floured board with a floured rolling pin, roll out the dough into a 16- to 18-inch round. Fold the dough in quarters or roll over the rolling pin and unroll or unfold onto a nonstick or lightly greased 10-inch round cake pan with the dough hanging over the sides all around. Mound the cheese filling in the center. Draw up the sides, pleating all around. Gather the ends in the center and twist firmly to make a knob, enclosing the package.
5. Let rise in a draftfree place 20 minutes. Bake 20 to 30 minutes, or until the bread is deep brown.

Romanian Cheese and Herb Bread

Romanians make this robust, moist bread with the local sheep's milk cheese, Brynza. If it is not available, use feta cheese for a bread bold enough to serve with thick soups or strong beer.

SMALL LOAF (1 POUND)	INGREDIENTS	LARGE LOAF (1½ POUNDS)
1½ teaspoons	active dry yeast	2¼ teaspoons
1¾ cups	bread flour	2⅔ cups
½ cup	whole wheat flour	¾ cup
1 teaspoon	salt	1½ teaspoons
1 tablespoon	sugar	1½ tablespoons
1 teaspoon	fennel seeds	1½ teaspoons
1 teaspoon	caraway seeds	1½ teaspoons
⅛ teaspoon	cayenne	¼ teaspoon
½ cup	crumbled Brynza or feta cheese	¾ cup
⅔ cup	water	1 cup

Add all ingredients in the order suggested by your bread machine manual and process on the bread cycle according to the manufacturer's directions.

Russian Pot Cheese and Dill Bread

Who would guess that raw onions help give this close-grained sandwich bread its mellow flavor and moist, light texture. It is packed with protein and turns sliced meats and smoked fish into great sandwiches. In the machine, the dough will look very dry during the first few minutes of kneading. As soon as the onions release their juices, it will all come together in a soft dough.

SMALL LOAF (1 POUND)	INGREDIENTS	LARGE LOAF (1½ POUNDS)
1½ teaspoons	active dry yeast	2 ¼ teaspoons
1¾ cups	bread flour	2 ⅔ cups
½ cup	rye flour	¾ cup
1 tablespoon	sugar	1½ tablespoons
½ teaspoon	salt	¾ teaspoon
1 tablespoon	chopped fresh dill weed	1½ tablespoons
	or	
1 teaspoon	dried dill weed	1½ teaspoons
1 tablespoon	vegetable oil	1½ tablespoons
½ cup	chopped raw onion	¾ cup
½ cup	pot cheese (or well-drained cottage cheese)	¾ cup
½ cup	water	¾ cup

Add all ingredients in the order suggested by your bread machine manual and process on the bread cycle according to the manufacturer's directions.

Bialies

The bialy, first cousin to the bagel, comes from the Jewish communities of Eastern Europe. It is softer, easier to make, and at least as much fun to eat as a bagel. Slice horizontally and fill with cream cheese and smoked salmon or with cream cheese or butter alone.

Yield: 8 bialies

DOUGH

---

2 teaspoons	active dry yeast
2 cups	bread flour
1 tablespoon	sugar
1 teaspoon	salt
1 tablespoon	vegetable oil
1 cup	water

TOPPING

½ cup	chopped onion
2 tablespoons	poppy seeds
1 tablespoon	vegetable oil

1. Add all ingredients for the dough in the order suggested by your bread machine manual and process on the dough cycle according to the manufacturer's directions.

2. For the topping, place the onions in a small saucepan with 1 cup of water. Bring to a boil and remove from the heat; drain. Mix the onions with the poppy seeds and oil.

3. At the end of the dough cycle, remove the dough from the machine. Divide into 8 equal pieces. On a floured board with a floured rolling pin, roll out each piece into a 4-inch round. Dip each side in flour and place on a lightly greased baking sheet. Grease the bottom of a 2½- to 3-inch glass. Press an indentation in the center of each bialy with the glass; do not cut all the way through the dough. Sprinkle the onion mixture over each bialy, leaving at least a ½-inch border without any topping and trapping lots of onions and poppy seeds in the indentation.

4. Let the bialies rise uncovered in a draftfree place 30 minutes. Meanwhile, preheat the oven to 375 degrees. Bake 15 to 20 minutes, until lightly golden but not crisp.

Slavic Potato Bread

This moist and tangy bread stands up well to borscht or any substantial vegetable soup, goulash, or roast beef. Any dish that tastes good with an assertive red wine will be better with potato bread.

SMALL LOAF (1 POUND)	INGREDIENTS	LARGE LOAF (1½ POUNDS)
½ cup	ricotta or cottage cheese	¾ cup
1¼ teaspoons	active dry yeast	2 teaspoons
1¾ cups	bread flour	2⅔ cups
½ teaspoon	grated nutmeg	¾ teaspoon
½ teaspoon	salt	¾ teaspoon
⅛ teaspoon	cayenne	¼ teaspoon
½ cup	mashed potatoes	¾ cup
1	whole egg	1
0	egg yolk	1
¼ cup	water	⅓ cup

1. Drain the cheese in a sieve lined with cheesecloth or a sturdy paper towel for 30 minutes. Discard the liquid.

2. Add all ingredients, including the drained cheese, in the order suggested by your bread machine manual and process on the bread cycle according to the manufacturer's directions.

Polish Poppy Seed Bread

This fruity, barely sweet and tart tea bread will appeal to everyone's mother. It is filled with so many good fruits and nuts and seeds that it is best on its own.

SMALL LOAF (1 POUND)	INGREDIENTS	LARGE LOAF (1½ POUNDS)
1½ teaspoons	active dry yeast	2¼ teaspoons
2 cups	bread flour	3 cups
2 tablespoons	powdered milk	3 tablespoons
1 teaspoon	salt	1½ teaspoons
2 tablespoons	poppy seeds	3 tablespoons
1 tablespoon	grated grapefruit or orange zest	1½ tablespoons
3 tablespoons	honey	¼ cup
2 tablespoons	butter	3 tablespoons
1	whole egg	1
0	egg yolk	1
¾ cup	water	1 cup plus 1 tablespoon
¼ cup	raisins	⅓ cup
¼ cup	sliced almonds	⅓ cup

1. Add all ingredients except the raisins and almonds in the order suggested by your bread machine manual and process on the bread cycle according to the manufacturer's directions.

2. At the beeper (or at the end of the first kneading in the Panasonic, Sanyo, and National), add the raisins and almonds.

Bulgarian Bird of Paradise Bread

Olives, ham, and cheese decorate this round loaf that is large enough to feed a houseful. It looks modern, but it is an old ethnic celebration bread for weddings or religious festivals. It makes a welcome contribution to a potluck supper. For vegetarians, substitute cherry tomatoes for the ham.

Yield: 1 (12-inch) round loaf

DOUGH	
2	eggs
1½ teaspoons	active dry yeast
2 cups	bread flour
1½ teaspoons	sugar
1 teaspoon	salt
¼ cup	plain yogurt
¼ cup	water

TOPPING	
6 ounces	Brynza or feta cheese
2 ounces	unsliced ham
12	pimiento-stuffed green olives

1. Beat the eggs until blended. Set aside and reserve 1 tablespoon of the beaten egg.
2. Add all ingredients for the dough, including the remaining beaten eggs, in the order suggested by your bread machine manual and process on the dough cycle according to the manufacturer's directions.

3. At the end of the dough cycle, remove the dough from the machine. Preheat the oven to 350 degrees.

4. On a floured board with a floured rolling pin, roll out the dough into a 12-inch circle. Place on a greased baking sheet. Brush with the reserved egg. Cut the cheese into 4 thin (¼ inch thick) triangles, about 3 inches on each side. Arrange them equidistant on the bread with a point of each triangle pointing toward the center and the sides about 1 inch from the edge of the dough. Cut the ham into ½-inch cubes and place them between the cheese triangles, again leaving an inch around the edge. Arrange the olives to make a circle in the center.

5. Let rise in a draftfree place 40 minutes. Bake 30 minutes, or until golden brown.

Latvian Piragi

Piragi—*the Latvian version of* pirogi—*are robust hors d'oeuvres. If you roll the dough very thin and give the piragi enough time to rise, the wrappers will be airy and tender. Dip them in horseradish mixed with an equal measure of sour cream or yogurt. Traditionally they are drizzled with melted butter and served with soup.*

Yield: 24 small piragi

DOUGH

2 teaspoons	active dry yeast
2 cups	bread flour
2 tablespoons	powdered milk
1 tablespoon	sugar
1 teaspoon	salt
¼ cup	vegetable oil
1	egg
½ cup	water

FILLING

1	medium onion, chopped
1 teaspoon	vegetable oil
1	garlic clove, minced
½ pound	ground beef
½ cup	mashed potatoes
¼ teaspoon	salt
⅛ teaspoon	ground black pepper

1. Add all ingredients for the dough in the order suggested by your bread machine manual and process on the dough cycle according to the manufacturer's directions. **2.** Meanwhile, sauté the onion in the oil in a nonstick skillet over medium-high heat until translucent, about 3 minutes. Add the garlic and ground beef. Cook, stirring to break up any lumps, until the meat is no longer pink, 2 to 3 minutes. Remove from the heat and stir in the mashed potatoes, salt, and pepper. Let cool to room temperature.

3. At the end of the dough cycle, remove the dough from the machine. On a floured board with a floured rolling pin, roll out the dough ⅛ inch thick or thinner. Be sure it is not sticking to the work surface. With a 2- to 2½-inch thick cookie cutter or glass, cut out circles. Place about ½ tablespoon of filling on the left side of each circle, about ¼ inch in from the edge. Fold the right side over left and pinch the edges tightly together to seal. Gather up the scraps, reroll, and cut and fill with any remaining filling.

4. Let rise in a draftfree place 15 minutes. In a large nonstick skillet, cook the piragi in 2 to 3 batches over medium-low heat 8 to 10 minutes, or until golden brown. Turn and cook until golden on the other side, 5 to 7 minutes. Eat warm.

Jewish Rye Bread

SMALL LOAF (1 POUND)	INGREDIENTS	LARGE LOAF (1½ POUNDS)
SPONGE		
½ teaspoon	active dry yeast	¾ teaspoon
¾ cup	rye flour	1 cup plus 2 tablespoons
½ cup	sourdough starter*	¾ cup
¾ cup	water	1 cup plus 2 tablespoons
BREAD		
¾ teaspoon	active dry yeast	1¼ teaspoons
1½ cups	bread flour	2¼ cups
1 teaspoon	salt	1½ teaspoons
2 teaspoons	sugar	1 tablespoon
2 teaspoons	caraway seeds	1 tablespoon
1 tablespoon	vegetable oil	1½ tablespoons

1. At least 4 and up to 8 hours before you plan to put this bread into the bread machine, mix together the ingredients for the sponge. Cover and let stand at room temperature.

2. After at least 4 hours, when the sponge has developed air bubbles, add all of the bread ingredients and the sponge in the order suggested by your bread machine manual. Process on the bread cycle according to the manufacturer's directions.

*After measuring out what is needed for this recipe, be sure to replenish your sourdough starter with equal amounts of flour and water.

Polish Babka

SMALL LOAF (1 POUND)	INGREDIENTS	LARGE LOAF (1½ POUNDS)
¾ cup plus 2 tablespoons	milk	1¼ cups
½ cup	bread flour	¾ cup
1 teaspoon	active dry yeast	1½ teaspoons
1½ cups	bread flour	2¼ cups
3 tablespoons	sugar	¼ cup
½ teaspoon	salt	¾ teaspoon
1 tablespoon	grated lemon zest	1½ tablespoons
½ teaspoon	vanilla extract	¾ teaspoon
4 tablespoons	unsalted butter	6 tablespoons
3	egg yolks	4
½ cup	golden raisins	¾ cup
½ teaspoon	ground cinnamon	¾ teaspoon
1 teaspoon	brown sugar	1½ teaspoons

1. Bring the milk to a boil. Stir in ½ cup flour if you are using the small machine, ¾ cup for the larger. Cook over medium heat, stirring constantly, until the mixture looks like mashed potatoes. Remove from the heat and let cool.

2. Add the milk mixture and all other ingredients except the raisins, cinnamon, and brown sugar to the bread machine in the order suggested by your bread machine manual. Process on the bread cycle according to the manufacturer's directions.

3. Mix the raisins with the cinnamon and brown sugar and add at the beeper (or at the end of the first kneading in the Panasonic, Sanyo, and National).

4. At the end of the entire cycle, let the babka cool 30 minutes in the open machine to keep the sides of the bread firm and straight.

Hungarian Cream Coffee Cake

If you ever forget to buy a birthday cake, here is one you make yourself. Since there are three layers of dough and two of filling, this loaf looks like a high layer cake when cut. My mother loves this cake for her birthday.

Yield: 1 (9-inch) round loaf

DOUGH

2 teaspoons	active dry yeast
2½ cups	bread flour
3 tablespoons	sugar
1 teaspoon	salt
4 tablespoons	unsalted butter
1	egg
½ cup	milk
½ cup	heavy cream

FILLING AND GLAZE

2 tablespoons	unsweetened cocoa powder
¼ cup	granulated sugar
¼ cup	chopped walnuts
4 tablespoons	melted unsalted butter
½ cup	confectioners' sugar
2 tablespoons	milk

1. Add all ingredients for the dough in the order suggested by your bread machine manual and process on the dough cycle according to the manufacturer's directions.
2. At the end of the dough cycle, remove the dough from the machine. Grease a 9-inch round cake pan or pie tin. Divide the dough into 3 equal pieces. On a floured surface with a floured rolling pin, roll out each piece of dough into a 9-inch round.
3. Place the first piece of dough in the bottom of the cake pan. Sprinkle half of the cocoa, granulated sugar, and walnuts over the dough. Drizzle on half the melted butter. Add another dough round. Sprinkle on the remaining cocoa, granulated sugar, and nuts and drizzle on the remaining butter. Top with the last round of dough. Let rise 40 minutes in a draftfree place. Meanwhile, preheat the oven to 350 degrees.
4. Bake 45 minutes. Let cool 15 minutes, then unmold and let cool completely, bottom side-up.
5. Mix together the confectioners' sugar and milk to make a glaze. Pour over the cooled cake.

Hungarian Doughnuts
(Fank)

Timing is important with fank, *since they are at their crisp, airy best as soon as they are cooked. It is fine to make the dough up to several hours ahead, cut out the doughnuts—which do not have a hole in the center—and refrigerate them, covered, until an hour before serving. Then they can be enjoyed freshly fried. Just be sure to allow time for them to rise before frying. The vanilla sugar on top makes sure you know these are Hungarian.*

Yield: 20 to 24 fank

2 teaspoons	active dry yeast
2½ cups	bread flour
2 tablespoons	sugar
½ teaspoon	salt
1 tablespoon	grated lemon zest
2	egg yolks
½ cup	sour cream or plain yogurt
¾ cup	milk
½ cup	raisins
2 to 4 cups	vegetable oil, for frying
¼ cup	vanilla sugar*

1. Add all ingredients except the raisins, oil, and vanilla sugar in the order suggested by your bread machine manual and process on the dough cycle according to the manufacturer's directions. At the beeper, add the raisins. If your machine does not have a beeper during the dough cycle, add the raisins about 15 minutes after you start the machine.

2. When the dough cycle ends, remove the dough from the machine. On a floured surface with a floured rolling pin, roll out the dough into a 12-by-18-inch rectangle. Cut into 2- to 2½-inch circles with a glass or biscuit cutter.

3. Place on a greased baking sheet, cover loosely, and let rise 30 minutes, or until doubled in size. You may refrigerate the doughnuts at this point. If you do, give them enough time to come to room temperature and rise after they are removed from the refrigerator.

4. In a deep-fat fryer or large saucepan, heat the oil to 365 degrees. Fry 3 or 4 doughnuts at a time 10 to 15 seconds on one side until golden. Turn carefully and fry the other side until golden. Drain on crumpled brown paper bags or newspaper covered with a sheet of paper towel. Sprinkle vanilla sugar over the doughnuts and serve at once.

*See note on page 49.

Polish Jelly Doughnuts

We think of jelly doughnuts as American, but they actually originated in Europe. These small Polish jelly doughnuts are perfect party food—for children or adults. Nothing breaks the ice like warm jelly doughnuts. How cool can the most sophisticated person be with a touch of red preserves at the corner of her mouth or a dab of powdered sugar on his nose?

Yield: 24 small doughnuts

DOUGH

---

2 teaspoons	active dry yeast
2 cups	bread flour
⅓ cup	confectioners' sugar
½ teaspoon	salt
1 teaspoon	vanilla extract
2	eggs
½ cup	milk

FILLING AND TOPPING

¼ cup	raspberry, cherry, or apricot preserves
2 to 4 cups	vegetable oil, for frying
¼ cup	confectioners' sugar

1. Add all ingredients for the dough in the order suggested by your bread machine manual and process on the dough cycle according to the manufacturer's directions. **2.** When the dough cycle ends, remove the dough from the machine. On a floured board with a floured rolling pin, roll out the dough into a 10-by-15-inch rectangle. With a 2½-inch biscuit cutter or glass, cut out 24 rounds. With your finger make an indentation in the center of each round and place ½ teaspoon of preserves in each, being careful not to let the preserves go near the edge. Pull up the edges and pinch firmly together to totally enclose the preserves. Place seam sides-down on a greased baking sheet. Cover loosely and let rise 1 hour.
3. In a deep-fat fryer, wok, or large saucepan, heat the oil to 365 degrees. Fry 3 or 4 jelly doughnuts at a time 10 to 15 seconds on each side, until golden. Drain quickly on crumpled brown paper bags or on several layers of newspaper covered with a sheet of paper towel.
4. Sprinkle confectioners' sugar over the doughnuts.

Russian Easter Bread
(Kulich)

For Easter in pre-Communist Russia, this sweet bread was usually served with a molded dessert of eggs and heavy cream called pashka. *Between them, they contain an artillery of eggs. Serve small pieces as a special treat.*

SMALL LOAF (1 POUND)	INGREDIENTS	LARGE LOAF (1½ POUNDS)
½ cup	milk	¾ cup
6 tablespoons	unsalted butter	9 tablespoons
1½ teaspoons	active dry yeast	2¼ teaspoons
2 cups	bread flour	3 cups
3 tablespoons	granulated sugar	¼ cup
1 tablespoon	grated lemon zest	1½ tablespoons
1 teaspoon	salt	1½ teaspoons
1 teaspoon	vanilla extract	1½ teaspoons
3	egg yolks	4
½ cup	raisins	¾ cup
3 tablespoons	amber or dark rum	¼ cup
¼ cup	chopped candied fruit	⅓ cup
1 cup	confectioners' sugar	1½ cups
2 tablespoons	lemon juice	3 tablespoons

1. In a small saucepan, heat the milk until it bubbles around the edges. Remove from the heat. Cut the butter into tablespoons and add to the hot milk. Stir until dissolved. Let cool to room temperature.

2. Add the buttered milk, yeast, flour, granulated sugar, lemon zest, salt, vanilla, and egg yolks in the order suggested by your bread machine manual and process on the basic or sweet bread cycle according to the manufacturer's directions.

3. Soak the raisins in the rum 10 minutes; drain well.

4. At the beeper (or at the end of the first kneading in the Panasonic, Sanyo, and National), add the raisins and candied fruit.

5. At the end of the baking cycle, let the bread cool in the open machine ½ hour to keep the crust strong. Remove.

6. Mix together the confectioners' sugar and lemon juice. Pour over the bread, letting it drip down the sides.

Hamantaschen

Purim, the joyful Jewish holiday that celebrates victory over a cruel tyrant, is the time for hamantaschen. *These triangular pastries filled with sweetened prunes or poppy seeds represent the tricornered hat of the wicked despot Haman. The holiday falls in late winter, but* hamantaschen *make lovely treats year round.*

Yield: 24 hamantaschen

FILLING

¼ cup	water
½ cup	poppy seeds
2 tablespoons	honey
2 tablespoons	sugar
1 tablespoon	grated orange zest
1 tablespoon	orange juice

DOUGH

2 teaspoons	active dry yeast
2 cups	bread flour
½ teaspoon	salt
¼ cup	sugar
2	eggs
2 tablespoons	vegetable oil
½ cup	water

---

1. Bring the water to a boil. Add the poppy seeds, honey, and sugar and return to a boil. Remove from the heat and add the orange zest and orange juice. Let cool to room temperature.

2. Add all ingredients for the dough in the order suggested by your bread machine manual and process on the dough cycle according to the manufacturer's directions.

3. When the dough cycle ends, remove the dough from the machine. Preheat the oven to 350 degrees.

4. On a floured surface with a floured rolling pin, roll out the dough into a 12-by-8-inch rectangle. With a 2-inch cookie cutter or glass, cut 24 rounds. Place them on a lightly greased baking sheet. Put ½ teaspoon of filling in the center of each circle. Bring up the edges and pinch tightly closed at 3 places to make a tricorner with ½ inch of the center open to show the filling.

5. Let rise, lightly covered, in a draftfree place 30 minutes. Bake 15 to 20 minutes, or until golden.

Bohemian Kolachy

The smaller you make these pristine little pastries, the more elegant they will be and the faster they will disappear. Late at night with wine, or early in the morning with coffee, kolachy *are as satisfying as Danish pastries and as delicate as cookies.*

Yield: 30 kolachy

FILLING

1 cup	pitted prunes or dried apricots
2 cups	boiling water
2 tablespoons	sugar
½ teaspoon	ground cinnamon

DOUGH

1½ teaspoons	active dry yeast
2 cups	bread flour
¼ teaspoon	sugar
½ teaspoon	salt
2 teaspoons	grated lemon zest
4 tablespoons	unsalted butter
1	egg
½ cup	heavy cream
⅓ cup	water

1. Add prunes or apricots to boiling water. Let cool to room temperature; drain. Puree the dried fruit in a food processor with the sugar and cinnamon.

2. Add all ingredients for the dough in the order suggested by your bread machine manual and process on the dough cycle according to the manufacturer's directions.

3. At the end of the dough cycle, remove the dough from the machine. Preheat the oven to 350 degrees.

4. On a floured surface with a floured rolling pin, roll out the dough into a 10-by-12-inch rectangle, about ¼ inch thick. Cut out rounds of dough with a 2-inch cookie cutter or glass. Place rounds on a lightly greased baking sheet. With your finger, press an indentation in the center of each round. Add 1 teaspoon of fruit filling to each depression.

5. Let rise, loosely covered, in a draftfree place 20 minutes. Bake 15 minutes, or until golden brown.

Russian Krendel

Celebrating saints' days in old Russia required krendel, *a sweet, rich, and fragrant pastry twist. It is as delectable first thing in the morning with coffee as it is at midday or late at night with hot chocolate or spiced cider.*

Yield: 1 krendel

1½ teaspoons	active dry yeast
2 cups	bread flour
2 tablespoons	powdered milk
3 tablespoons	sugar
½ teaspoon	salt
1 tablespoon	grated lemon zest
1 teaspoon	vanilla extract
6 tablespoons	unsalted butter
3	egg yolks
½ cup	water
1	egg white
2 tablespoons	sliced blanched almonds

1. Add all ingredients except the egg white and almonds in the order suggested by your bread machine manual and process on the dough cycle according to the manufacturer's directions.

2. At the end of the dough cycle, remove the dough from the machine. Preheat the oven to 400 degrees.

3. Roll out the dough into a 30-inch rope, thicker in the center and thinner at the ends. Make a circle, crossing the rope 3 inches from the ends. Twist the 2 ends at the 3-inch point to secure them, and tuck the ends under the opposite sides of the circle to make a pretzel shape. Put the *krendel* on a lightly greased baking sheet. Brush with the egg white and sprinkle the sliced almonds on top. Let rise 20 to 30 minutes until doubled in size.

4. Place the *krendel* in the oven and immediately reduce the heat to 350 degrees. Bake 15 to 20 minutes, or until golden brown.

Hungarian Kugelhopf

This high, handsome cake is a picture-book coffee cake. Both rich and light, it contains a little chocolate, which sparks the buttery taste. Serve fresh to your fanciest, most jaded guests. Toast any leftovers.

Yield: 1 (10-inch) ring cake

DOUGH

1 tablespoon	active dry yeast
3 cups	bread flour
¼ cup	sugar
1 stick (½ cup)	unsalted butter
¼ teaspoon	salt
4	egg yolks
2 tablespoons	sour cream
1 cup	milk

FILLING AND TOPPING

3 tablespoons	unsweetened cocoa powder
¼ cup	sugar
½ cup	raisins
1 tablespoon	vanilla sugar*

1. Add all ingredients for the dough in the order suggested by your bread machine manual and process on the dough cycle according to the manufacturer's directions.
2. At the end of the dough cycle, remove the dough from the machine. Grease a kugelhopf or bundt pan or any 10-inch tube pan.
3. On a floured surface, press out this soft dough with your hands into a 12-inch square. Sprinkle the cocoa, sugar, and raisins over the dough. Roll up like a jelly roll and place in kugelhopf pan, seam side-up. Cover and let rise in a draftfree place 1 hour, or until doubled in size. Preheat the oven to 350 degrees.
4. Bake 40 minutes. Let cool 15 minutes, then turn out of the pan. Sprinkle vanilla sugar on top.

*Vanilla sugar is powdered or confectioners' or XXX sugar with a piece of vanilla bean buried in it. Keep vanilla sugar in a covered container or in a sugar shaker covered with plastic. Let the vanilla sugar stand a few days before using to develop flavor. As you use it, add more confectioners' sugar to the vanilla bean.

Chapter Two
Breads of the Mediterranean

In France, Italy, Spain, Portugal, and Greece every village once had its own special bread, as it traditionally had its unique cheese or specially shaped pasta. Now these breads have spread from town to town and into the large cities. In Milan, you can find all of the breads of Italy, the rustic whole wheats, the heavily crusted salt-free Tuscan breads, breads shaped like doves for Easter, skinny *grissini* (bread sticks), to eat like chips. In France, the breads of Paris have reached the countryside, while Parisians revere the sourdough of country peasant loaves.

The French make the lightest and richest of breads: brioche. Nothing makes this classic as well as the bread machine—not a mixer, a food processor, mixing by hand, or even a Frenchman. Whether you make a brioche loaf, chocolate brioche, or classic individual brioche, with the bread machine, you can be sure it will be sublime. That's the good news; now the bad. Croissants should not be made in a bread machine. The dough for croissants is not kneaded, it is just barely mixed, so this is one recipe you should save for a rainy day to do by hand.

You can, however, make great round French *boules*, Greek herb breads, Portuguese corn bread, and Spanish breads to serve as *tapas*, or hors d'oeuvres. And the best news is that most of the breads of the Mediterranean are low in fat and cholesterol and full of flavor.

French Sandwich Bread
(Pain de Mie)

Cool and slice pain de mie not more than ¼ inch thick for canapés or sandwiches. It tastes best when buttered and topped or filled with anchovy or tuna pastes, sliced cucumbers, watercress or radishes, or just peanut butter and jelly.

SMALL LOAF (1 POUND)	INGREDIENTS	LARGE LOAF (1½ POUNDS)
1 teaspoon	active dry yeast	1½ teaspoons
2 cups	bread flour	3 cups
2 teaspoons	sugar	1 tablespoon
1 teaspoon	salt	1½ teaspoons
2 tablespoons	vegetable oil	3 tablespoons
¾ cup plus 2 tablespoons	water	1¼ cups

Add all ingredients in the order suggested by your bread machine manual and process on the bread cycle according to the manufacturer's directions.

French Boule

Boule *means "ball" in French. This big, round loaf is made from the same dough as the skinny* baguette *and the even thinner* ficelle. *Slice the* boule *½ inch thick for sandwiches or toast, or simply butter it. The crunchy crust contrasts brilliantly with the soft but not fluffy inside. Before you bake the bread, tear off a nubbin of dough and save it wrapped and refrigerated. Add it to your next loaf in a day or two to enhance the flavor of the bread; do not keep it more than a week.*

SMALL LOAF (1 POUND)	INGREDIENTS	LARGE LOAF (1½ POUNDS)
1¼ teaspoons	active dry yeast	2 teaspoons
2 cups	bread flour	3 cups
2 teaspoons	sugar	1 tablespoon
1 teaspoon	salt	1½ teaspoons
2 teaspoons	vegetable oil	1 tablespoon
¾ cup plus 2 tablespoons	water	1¼ cups

1. Add all ingredients for the dough in the order suggested by your bread machine manual and process on the dough cycle according to the manufacturer's directions.
2. At the end of the dough cycle, remove the dough from the machine. Shape dough into a large ball, pulling the edges of the dough underneath and pinching them together to help smooth the top and eliminate air pockets. Cover loosely and let rise in a draftfree place 40 minutes. Preheat the oven to 400 degrees.
3. Sprinkle 2 or 3 teaspoons of additional flour on top. With a single-edged razor or a sharp knife, cut a cross on top of the bread. Place in the oven and immediately reduce the heat to 375 degrees. Bake 30 to 40 minutes, or until the bread sounds hollow when the bottom is tapped.

Parisian Sourdough Bread

This loaf is really sour and really dense. The slow rising of the sponge method produces a bread that stays fresh longer and has a finer grain. It stands up to spicy tomato sauce, boeuf bourguignon, *or vegetable ragout.*

SMALL LOAF (1 POUND)	INGREDIENTS	LARGE LOAF (1½ POUNDS)
SPONGE		
¾ teaspoon	active dry yeast	1¼ teaspoons
½ cup	bread flour	¾ cup
⅓ cup	whole wheat flour	½ cup
½ cup	sourdough starter*	¾ cup
⅔ cup	water	1 cup
DOUGH		
1 cup	bread flour	1½ cups
½ teaspoon	salt	¾ teaspoon

1. In a medium bowl, mix all ingredients for the sponge until well blended. Cover the sponge and let stand in a draftfree place 1 hour.

2. Add the sponge and the flour and salt for the dough to your bread machine. Process on the bread cycle according to the manufacturer's directions.

*After measuring out what is needed for this recipe, be sure to replenish your sourdough starter with equal amounts of flour and water.

French Sourdough Whole Wheat Bread

This strong, honest loaf tastes of wheat, especially if you prepare it with coarsely ground grain. Make sandwiches with a highly seasoned pâté or full-flavored cheese or top a slice with ratatouille or Roquefort cheese and pear. It makes grainy, nutty toast.

SMALL LOAF (1 POUND)	INGREDIENTS	LARGE LOAF (1½ POUNDS)
1½ teaspoons	active dry yeast	2¼ teaspoons
1 cup	bread flour	1½ cups
1¼ cups	whole wheat flour	1¾ cups
1 teaspoon	salt	1½ teaspoons
2 tablespoons	honey	3 tablespoons
½ cup	sourdough starter*	¾ cup
½ cup	water	¾ cup

Add all ingredients in the order suggested by your bread machine manual and process according to the manufacturer's directions on the whole wheat cycle or the longest bread cycle on your machine.

*After measuring out what is needed for this recipe, be sure to replenish your sourdough starter with equal amounts of flour and water.

Semolina Sourdough Bread

Dense and crusty, perfect for sandwiches with salami or prosciutto or mozzarella cheese and roasted vegetables, this semolina bread also goes well with an antipasto or a thick, rich soup. The top will split a little, giving the machine loaf an earthy look. Semolina is a golden, very high gluten flour used mainly for pasta.

SMALL LOAF (1 POUND)	INGREDIENTS	LARGE LOAF (1½ POUNDS)
1 teaspoon	active dry yeast	1½ teaspoons
1¾ cups	semolina flour	2¼ cups
2 teaspoons	sugar	1 tablespoon
1 teaspoon	salt	1½ teaspoons
2 tablespoons	yellow cornmeal	3 tablespoons
½ cup	sourdough starter*	¾ cup
⅔ cup	water	¾ cup plus 2 tablespoons
1 teaspoon	sesame seeds (optional)	1½ teaspoons

1. Add all ingredients except the sesame seeds in the order suggested by your bread machine manual and process on the bread cycle according to the manufacturer's directions.

2. If you wish to top the bread with sesame seeds, sprinkle them on the bread during the last rising, being careful not to have them fall outside the container pan and into the machine body.

*After measuring out what is needed for this recipe, be sure to replenish your sourdough starter with equal amounts of flour and water.

Italian Skinny Bread Sticks
(Grissini)

These skinny, crispy sticks look and taste festive when poked into a basket of crudités or tied in a bunch with ribbon. There is no simpler snack to accompany a glass of wine or juice.

Yield: 16 bread sticks

1½ teaspoons	active dry yeast
2 cups	bread flour
1 teaspoon	salt
¼ teaspoon	coarsely ground black pepper
2 tablespoons	olive oil
¾ cup plus 2 tablespoons	water

1. Add all ingredients for the dough in the order suggested by your bread machine manual and process on the dough cycle according to the manufacturer's directions. Preheat the oven to 400 degrees.

2. At the end of the dough cycle, remove the dough from the machine. Divide into 16 equal pieces. On a floured board with floured hands, roll each piece into a thin stick at least 10 inches long.

3. Place the sticks of dough 1 inch apart on a greased baking sheet. Do not let rise. Bake immediately 10 to 15 minutes, until golden. Watch carefully: The thinner the sticks, the faster they will bake—and burn.

Mediterranean Multigrain Bread

This moist, nutty, full-flavored bread tastes so good that you can forget how healthy it is, full of fiber and vitamins and minerals. Eat it with minestrone or any kind of soup, in a sandwich filled with tunafish or chicken salad or roasted vegetables, or toasted for breakfast.

SMALL LOAF (1 POUND)	INGREDIENTS	LARGE LOAF (1½ POUNDS)
1½ teaspoons	active dry yeast	2¼ teaspoons
1½ cups	bread flour	2¼ cups
½ cup	whole wheat flour	¾ cup
¼ cup	rye flour	⅓ cup
¼ cup	oatmeal	⅓ cup
½ teaspoon	salt	¾ teaspoon
¼ cup	chopped walnuts	⅓ cup
1 cup	water	1⅓ cups

Add all ingredients in the order suggested by your bread machine manual and process on the bread cycle according to the manufacturer's directions.

Salt-Free French Bread

The recipe for this soft, moist, sandwich bread is based on Bernard Clayton, Jr.'s bread without salt in his book The Breads of France. *Potatoes make the bread smoother and more delicate and help keep us from missing the salt.*

SMALL LOAF (1 POUND)	INGREDIENTS	LARGE LOAF (1½ POUNDS)
1 teaspoon	active dry yeast	1½ teaspoons
2 cups	bread flour	3 cups
2 tablespoons	mashed potato	3 tablespoons
2 tablespoons	powdered milk	3 tablespoons
1 tablespoon	sugar	1½ tablespoons
¾ cup plus 2 tablespoons	water	1¼ cups

Add all ingredients in the order suggested by your bread machine manual and process on the bread cycle according to the manufacturer's directions.

Salt-Free Tuscan Whole Wheat Bread

This dense, dark, low-calorie, no-fat bread needs only a little sugar-free jam for an excellent breakfast. The sourdough starter gives it interesting flavor and texture and keeps the bread moist in its saltless state. Thanks to Carol Fields' The Italian Baker *for inspiring this bread.*

SMALL LOAF (1 POUND)	INGREDIENTS	LARGE LOAF (1½ POUNDS)
1 teaspoon	active dry yeast	1½ teaspoons
¾ cup	bread flour	1 cup plus 2 tablespoons
1½ cups	whole wheat flour	2¼ cups
1 tablespoon	honey	1½ tablespoons
½ cup	sourdough starter*	¾ cup
½ cup	water	¾ cup plus 2 tablespoons

Add all ingredients in the order suggested by your bread machine manual and process on the bread cycle according to the manufacturer's directions.

*After measuring out what is needed for this recipe, be sure to replenish your sourdough starter with equal amounts of flour and water.

Portuguese Corn Bread
(Broa)

Light, grainy broa partners chili or a spicy stew or thick soup. Smear a fresh or toasted slice with butter or soft avocado and/or tomato, or ladle a fish stew over toasted broa.

SMALL LOAF (1 POUND)	INGREDIENTS	LARGE LOAF (1½ POUNDS)
1 cup	yellow cornmeal	1½ cups
1¼ cups	cold water	1¾ cups
1½ teaspoons	active dry yeast	2¼ teaspoons
1½ cups	bread flour	2¼ cups
2 teaspoons	sugar	1 tablespoon
¾ teaspoon	salt	1¼ teaspoons
1 tablespoon	olive oil	1½ tablespoons

1. Stir the cornmeal into ½ (¾) cup of the cold water until there are no lumps.
2. Add all ingredients in the order suggested by your bread machine manual and process on the bread cycle according to the manufacturer's directions.

Greek Oregano and Lemon Bread

You can smell lemons and oregano at sea as you come near the Greek islands that are not too stony to support growth. Oregano will grow between the cracks in rocks. This bread is comfortable with broiled or sauced fish. Toast, rub with garlic, and float in chicken or egg-lemon soup.

SMALL LOAF (1 POUND)	INGREDIENTS	LARGE LOAF (1½ POUNDS)
1½ teaspoons	active dry yeast	2¼ teaspoons
1⅔ cups	bread flour	2½ cups
½ cup	whole wheat flour	¾ cup
1 teaspoon	salt	1½ teaspoons
2 teaspoons	sugar	1 tablespoon
1 tablespoon	grated lemon zest	1½ tablespoons
2 teaspoons	dried oregano	1 tablespoon
2 tablespoons	olive oil	3 tablespoons
¾ cup plus 2 tablespoons	water	1¼ cups
1 tablespoon	lemon juice	1½ tablespoons

1. Add all ingredients except the lemon juice in the order suggested by your bread machine manual and process on the bread cycle according to the manufacturer's directions.

2. When the bread cycle is complete, open the machine and brush the bread with lemon juice.

Spanish Potato and Onion Bread

Potato and onion "tortilla," actually an omelet, is often one of the dishes in an array of tapas in Spanish bars. Changed into a bread, it makes a yummy hors d'oeuvre to nibble with sherry, cocktails, or soup. Serve in warm, fresh wedges or cut into fingers and toasted.

SMALL LOAF (1 POUND)	INGREDIENTS	LARGE LOAF (1½ POUNDS)
1½ teaspoons	active dry yeast	2¼ teaspoons
1⅔ cups	bread flour	2½ cups
½ cup	whole wheat flour	¾ cup
1 teaspoon	salt	1½ teaspoons
⅛ teaspoon	ground black pepper	¼ teaspoon
¾ cup	water	1 cup plus 2 tablespoons
⅔ cup	coarsely chopped onion	1 cup
2 tablespoons	olive oil	3 tablespoons
2	garlic cloves, minced	3
⅔ cup	finely diced peeled potato	1 cup

1. Add all ingredients except the onion, olive oil, garlic, and potatoes in the order suggested by your bread machine manual and process on the bread cycle according to the manufacturer's directions.

2. In a medium skillet, sauté the onion in the olive oil over medium heat until translucent, about 3 minutes. Add the garlic and potatoes and cook until the onion is just golden, 3 to 5 minutes. (The potatoes need not be cooked through at this point.)

3. At the beeper (or at the end of the first kneading in the Panasonic, Sanyo, and National), add the onions, garlic, and potatoes.

Sage Bread

Sage blooms all over Italy, and is particularly popular in the north. Making a chicken or turkey sandwich on sage bread is letting you have your bird and stuffing too, because this loaf tastes like stuffing. In fact, if there are any leftovers, they can be cubed and used for stuffing. The herbs, onions, and garlic in the bread turn even the plainest filling into an exciting sandwich, with no butter or mayonnaise necessary.

SMALL LOAF (1 POUND)	INGREDIENTS	LARGE LOAF (1½ POUNDS)
1½ teaspoons	active dry yeast	2¼ teaspoons
1¾ cups	bread flour	2⅔ cups
½ cup	whole wheat flour	¾ cup
1 teaspoon	sugar	1½ teaspoons
1 teaspoon	salt	1½ teaspoons
1 teaspoon	dried fresh sage	1½ teaspoons
	or	
2 teaspoons	minced fresh sage	1 tablespoon
1	garlic clove(s), minced	1½
¼ cup	minced onion	⅓ cup
1 tablespoon	vegetable oil	1½ tablespoons
¾ cup	water	1 cup plus 2 tablespoons

Add all ingredients in the order suggested by your bread machine manual and process on the bread cycle according to the manufacturer's directions.

Portuguese Sofrito Bread

In Portugal, slowly sautéed onions are called sofrito, *a deeply flavored beginning, or base, for dishes with rice or potatoes and for stews. The Italian* soffritto *adds herbs and celery; the Colombian adds annatto seeds. With roasted meat or chicken from any country, pass this Portuguese sofrito bread, or make an open-faced grilled cheese sandwich to remember.*

SMALL LOAF (1 POUND)	INGREDIENTS	LARGE LOAF (1½ POUNDS)
2	large onions	3
2 tablespoons	olive oil	3 tablespoons
1½ teaspoons	active dry yeast	2¼ teaspoons
2 cups	bread flour	3 cups
1 tablespoon	sugar	1½ tablespoons
1 teaspoon	salt	1½ teaspoons
½ cup	cooked rice	¾ cup
2 tablespoons	yellow cornmeal	3 tablespoons
⅓ cup	water	½ cup

1. Cut onions into ½-inch dice. Sauté slowly in olive oil until translucent and barely golden, about 15 minutes. Let cool.

2. Add all ingredients including the sautéed onions in the order suggested by your bread machine manual and process on the bread cycle according to the manufacturer's directions.

Tapenade Bread

Tapenade *is a coarse puree of olives, anchovies, and garlic that can fill and flavor eggs, pasta, or beans or be spread on toast. With the bread machine, the tapenade is incorporated into the bread, which can be toasted and used as a base for hors d'oeuvres. Since Tapenade Bread is garlicky, top it very simply with mild goat or cottage cheese or with hard-cooked eggs or cold meat.*

SMALL LOAF (1 POUND)	INGREDIENTS	LARGE LOAF (1½ POUNDS)
¼ cup	pitted black olives	⅓ cup
1	anchovy fillet(s)	2
2 tablespoons	capers, drained	3 tablespoons
1	crushed garlic clove(s)	1½
1 tablespoon	olive oil	1½ tablespoons
Large pinch	ground black pepper	⅛ teaspoon
1 teaspoon	active dry yeast	1½ teaspoons
2 cups	bread flour	3 cups
2 tablespoons	wheat bran	3 tablespoons
2 teaspoons	sugar	3 tablespoons
½ teaspoon	salt	¾ teaspoon
¾ cup	water	1 cup plus 2 tablespoons

1. In a food processor, puree the olives, anchovy fillet(s), capers, garlic, olive oil, and pepper. This is the tapenade.

2. Add all ingredients including the tapenade in the order suggested by your bread machine manual and process on the bread cycle according to the manufacturer's directions.

Calzone

Calzone is a giant turnover, a pizza folded in half. The filling is usually mainly cheese, with bits of vegetables or sausage. This calzone emphasizes spinach enriched with a little cheese. Bake miniature calzones as hors d'oeuvres, or share these larger calzones with friends at a casual party, or as the kids say, "It's not a party; we are just getting together."

Yield: 2 (10-inch) calzones

DOUGH

1½ teaspoons	active dry yeast
2 cups	bread flour
1½ teaspoons	salt
1 tablespoon	olive oil
1 teaspoon	sugar
¾ cup plus 2 tablespoons	water

FILLING

---

1 (10-ounce) package	frozen chopped spinach, thawed
1 cup	ricotta
2 tablespoons	grated Parmesan cheese
¼ teaspoon	garlic powder or flakes
½ teaspoon	salt
⅛ teaspoon	ground black pepper
1	whole egg white

1. Add all ingredients for the dough in the order suggested by your bread machine manual and process on the dough cycle according to the manufacturer's directions.
2. Preheat the oven to 375 degrees. In a cheesecloth or tea towel, squeeze the water out of the spinach. Mix the spinach with all the ingredients for the filling until well blended.
3. At the end of the dough cycle, remove the dough from the machine and divide it in half. On a floured board with a floured rolling pin, roll out each piece into a 10-inch circle. Place half the filling on one side of a circle. Pull the other side of the circle over the filling to make a semicircle. Pinch the edges together firmly to seal. Place on a greased baking sheet. With scissors, snip a small hole or two in the top. Repeat with the other calzone.
4. Let rise in a draftfree place 20 minutes. Bake 20 minutes, or until brown.

Brioche

If you can make brioche, you can bake anything. Rich with butter and eggs and so good looking, these brioches will make the baker proud and diners ecstatic. Start the night before, or make the dough and freeze it after shaping it into brioches. Let frozen brioche dough thaw in the refrigerator 3 hours, or overnight. Leftover brioches should be sliced and toasted. It makes canapés of pâté or smoked salmon and French toast without equal.

Yield: 8 brioches   Yield: 12 brioches

SMALL MACHINE	INGREDIENTS	LARGE MACHINE
DOUGH		
6 tablespoons	unsalted butter	1 stick (½ cup)
1¼ teaspoons	active dry yeast	1¾ teaspoons
1¼ cups	bread flour	1¾ cups plus 2 tablespoons
2 tablespoons	sugar	3 tablespoons
½ teaspoon	salt	¾ teaspoon
1	whole egg(s)	2
1	egg yolk	1
¼ cup	water	⅓ cup
1	egg white, beaten	1

1. Cut butter into tablespoons and let warm to room temperature.

2. Add all ingredients except the butter and egg white in the order suggested by your bread machine manual and process on the dough cycle according to the manufacturer's directions.

3. After the dough has been kneading about 5 minutes, add a piece of butter. Close the machine and let it continue kneading about 1 minute. Add another piece of butter, close the lid, and let knead. Repeat this process until you have used all the butter. Let the dough cycle continue until it is complete. Do not rush the addition of the butter; it should be completely incorporated into the dough. For machines that stop when the lid is lifted, be sure the lid is firmly closed after each addition. At the end of the dough cycle, transfer the dough from the machine to a greased bowl, cover, and refrigerate at least 3 hours, or overnight.

4. Cut the dough into 8 pieces for the smaller batch, into 12 pieces for the larger. From each piece of dough, cut off a piece the size of a marble. Roll each of the larger pieces into a ball and place in a greased fluted brioche tin or in a muffin tin. Press a deep indentation in the center of each ball. Roll each of the marble-size pieces into a cone shape. Place each cone, point down, in a ball of brioche dough, so it fits into the indentation. Brush the beaten egg white over the brioches. Let rise 1 hour in a draftfree place, until double in size. Meanwhile, preheat the oven to 400 degrees.

5. Place the brioches in the oven and reduce the temperature to 350 degrees. Bake 20 minutes, or until brown. When the tins are cool enough to handle, remove the brioches. Serve warm or at room temperature.

Chocolate Brioche Loaf

When you have a bread as light and rich as brioche, adding chocolate could be gilding the lily. So I have reduced the butter slightly to let the bittersweet chocolate come through, while maintaining the volume and delicacy of the brioche. This is a sensuous treat—buttered or plain with coffee, tea, or milk.

SMALL LOAF (1 POUND)	INGREDIENTS	LARGE LOAF (1½ POUNDS)
1¼ teaspoons	active dry yeast	1¾ teaspoons
1¾ cups	bread flour	2⅔ cups
¼ cup	unsweetened cocoa powder	⅓ cup
¼ cup	sugar	⅓ cup
½ teaspoon	salt	¾ teaspoon
4 tablespoons	unsalted butter	6 tablespoons
2	whole eggs	3
⅓ cup	water	½ cup

Add all ingredients in the order suggested by your bread machine manual and process on the bread cycle according to the manufacturer's directions.

Apple Charlotte

A charlotte is not a bread, it is a dessert formed in a cylindrical mold, which has an outer crust of cake or, in this case, bread. Use any light, sweet bread, such as Tiramisu or Zabaglione Bread or one of the raisin breads, such as Welsh or Belgian.

Yield: 6 individual desserts

1	loaf of sweet bread baked in the bread machine
4 tablespoons	unsalted butter
6	apples
3 tablespoons	brown sugar
3 tablespoons	granulated sugar
2 tablespoons	bread flour or all-purpose flour
1 teaspoon	ground cinnamon
Pinch	ground cloves

1. Preheat the oven to 400 degrees. Trim the crust from the loaf and cut into ¼-inch slices. Melt the butter. Liberally brush both sides of each slice with butter.

2. Peel, core, and slice the apples. Cook in a covered pan over medium heat 10 minutes, or until tender. Uncover, remove from the heat, and stir in the brown sugar, granulated sugar, flour, cinnamon, and cloves.

3. Line 6 individual (8-ounce) dessert ramekins or heatproof custard cups with half of the buttered bread. Divide the apple mixture among the 6. Completely cover each ramekin with bread slices. Set on a baking sheet to catch any spillover.

4. Bake 20 to 25 minutes, or until the tops are brown. Let cool slightly. Serve in the ramekins or let cool completely and unmold the desserts onto plates.

Portuguese Bread for the Epiphany
(Bolo Rei)

Finding the prize in the sweet bread on January 6, the Feast of the Epiphany, or of the three kings, means good fortune throughout the year. The bread is dense and almost as sweet without the lucky charm or coin.

Yield: 1 large bread

DOUGH

1½ teaspoons	active dry yeast
1⅔ cups	bread flour
¼ teaspoon	salt
3 tablespoons	sugar
1 tablespoon	grated orange zest
2 tablespoons	powdered milk
3 tablespoons	butter
1	egg
½ cup	water

FILLING AND TOPPING

¼ cup	raisins
¼ cup	chopped walnuts
2 tablespoons	port or other sweet wine
1	coin or toy charm
1	egg, beaten
6 to 12	candied cherries
12	blanched almonds

1. Add all ingredients for the dough in the order suggested by your bread machine manual and process on the dough cycle according to the manufacturer's directions.

2. Meanwhile, soak the raisins and nuts for the filling in the port or wine. At the end of the dough cycle, remove the dough from the machine.

3. On a floured board with a floured rolling pin, roll out the dough into a 6-by-18-inch rectangle. Drain the raisins and nuts and spread over the dough. Put a coin or charm on top. Roll up jelly-roll fashion from the long side. Place the dough on a baking sheet with the seam down and shape into a ring. Pinch the edges together to complete the circle.

4. Preheat the oven to 350 degrees. Brush the beaten egg over the top of the ring. Press cherries and almonds around the top in a decorative pattern. Let rise in a draftfree place about 30 minutes, or until doubled in size. Bake 20 to 30 minutes, or until golden.

Greek Christmas Bread
(Christopsomo)

Each staffer at the Greek Mission to the United Nations had a different Christopsomo *recipe, only the cross on top of the bread was common to all. This is a synthesis of the sweet celebration breads from Athens to Crete.*

SMALL LOAF (1 POUND)	INGREDIENTS	LARGE LOAF (1½ POUNDS)
1¼ teaspoons	active dry yeast	1¾ teaspoons
2 cups	bread flour	3 cups
1 teaspoon	salt	1½ teaspoons
1 tablespoon	grated lemon zest	1½ tablespoons
4 tablespoons	unsalted butter	6 tablespoons
2 tablespoons	honey	3 tablespoons
⅓ cup	sliced or slivered almonds	½ cup
1	whole egg	1
0	egg yolk	1
¾ cup	milk	1 cup plus 2 tablespoons

TOPPING

1 tablespoon	sliced or slivered almonds	1½ tablespoons
2 tablespoons	confectioners' sugar	3 tablespoons
4	whole almonds or walnut halves	4

1. Add all ingredients for the dough in the order suggested by your bread machine manual and process on the bread cycle according to the manufacturer's directions.
2. At the end of the kneading, during the final rising, sprinkle the 1 (1½) tablespoon(s) sliced almonds on top of the bread.
3. At the end of the baking cycle, when the bread is cool enough to handle, remove it from the machine. Mix the confectioners' sugar with a few drops of water, just enough to make a pourable glaze. Pour a cross on top of the bread. Place an almond or a walnut half on each end of the cross.

Semolina Baguette

Yield: 2 loaves   *Yield: 3 loaves*

SMALL LOAF (1 POUND)	INGREDIENTS	LARGE LOAF (1½ POUNDS)
DOUGH		
1½ teaspoons	active dry yeast	2¼ teaspoons
1 cup	bread flour	1½ cups
1 cup	semolina flour	1½ cups
1 tablespoon	sugar	1½ tablespoons
1 teaspoon	salt	1½ teaspoons
¾ cup plus 2 tablespoons	water	1¼ cups

1. Add all ingredients for the dough in the order suggested by your bread machine manual and process on the dough cycle according to the manufacturer's directions.
2. At the end of the dough cycle, remove the dough from the machine. Divide the dough in half (or in 3 pieces for the larger machines). Form each piece into a ball, cover, and let stand 15 minutes in a draftfree place.
3. Roll each piece of dough tightly into a 12- to 15-inch log with tapered ends. Place at least 2 inches apart on a lightly greased baking sheet(s). Cover loosely and let rise in a draftfree place 30 minutes. Meanwhile, preheat the oven to 400 degrees.
4. With a single-edged razor blade or a very sharp knife, gently make 3 diagonal slashes on the top of each loaf. Using a clean plant spritzer or water pistol, spray the breads with water and place in the oven. Immediately reduce the temperature to 375 degrees and bake 20 minutes.

Sourdough Hazelnut Rolls

Yield: 12 rolls   *Yield: 18 rolls*

SMALL LOAF (1 POUND)	INGREDIENTS	LARGE LOAF (1½ POUNDS)
1¼ teaspoons	active dry yeast	1¾ teaspoons
1¾ cups	bread flour	2⅔ cups
½ cup	sourdough starter*	¾ cup
2 tablespoons	powdered milk	3 tablespoons
1 tablespoon	sugar	1½ tablespoons
1 teaspoon	salt	1½ teaspoons
½ cup	chopped hazelnuts	¾ cup
1	whole egg	1
0	egg white	1
⅓ cup	water	½ cup

1. Add all ingredients for the dough in the order suggested by your bread machine manual and process on the dough cycle according to the manufacturer's directions. **2.** Preheat the oven to 375 degrees. When the dough cycle ends, remove the dough from the machine. Divide into 12 pieces for the smaller machine and 18 for the larger. On a floured board with floured hands, shape each piece into a 4-by-1-inch dinner roll. Place 1 inch apart on a greased baking sheet. Let rise, lightly covered, 25 minutes in a draftfree place. (Or let continue through the bread cycle for a soft, nutty loaf.) **3.** With a sharp knife or a single-edged razor blade, slash the top of each roll. Bake 15 to 20 minutes, until golden.

*After measuring out what is needed for this recipe, be sure to replenish your sourdough starter with equal amounts of flour and water.

Italian Easter Bread from Civitavecchia

This is a not-too-sweet bread to go with your morning cappuccino or afternoon tea. Its richness from the ricotta and spices does not interfere with its airiness. The Italian Baker by Carol Field first suggested this recipe.

SMALL LOAF (1 POUND)	INGREDIENTS	LARGE LOAF (1½ POUNDS)
1¼ teaspoons	active dry yeast	1¾ teaspoons
2 cups	bread flour	3 cups
¼ cup	water	⅓ cup
2 tablespoons	sugar	3 tablespoons
½ teaspoon	salt	¾ teaspoon
2 teaspoons	aniseed	1 tablespoon
2 teaspoons	grated lemon zest	1 tablespoon
3 tablespoons	ricotta	¼ cup
2	eggs	3
¼ cup	vegetable oil	⅓ cup

1. In a small bowl, mix the yeast with ¼ (⅓) cup of the flour and the ¼ (⅓) cup water. Cover and let rise in a draftfree place 1 hour.
2. Add all ingredients including the yeast mixture and the remaining flour in the order suggested by your bread machine manual and process on the bread cycle according to the manufacturer's directions.

Zabaglione Bread

Zabaglione is usually a custard or a custard sauce fragrant with marsala wine. This fat-free recipe reproduces the sweetness, flavor, and lightness of the dessert in a bread with a thick, sugary crust and a soft, moist center. Serve sliced plain or toasted with fruit or coffee.

SMALL LOAF (1 POUND)	INGREDIENTS	LARGE LOAF (1½ POUNDS)
1¼ teaspoons	active dry yeast	1¾ teaspoons
2 cups	bread flour	3 cups
3	egg whites	4
¼ cup	sugar	⅓ cup
½ teaspoon	salt	¾ teaspoon
⅓ cup	marsala wine	½ cup
¼ cup	water	⅓ cup

Add all ingredients in the order suggested by your bread machine manual and process on the bread cycle according to the manufacturer's directions.

Savarin

Savarin *is named after the ring-shaped mold from which it gets its shape. This light yet rich French dessert becomes a simple, easy triumph when made in the bread machine. The dough must be very wet and sticky to produce a very high, light cake. Note: If you are using a Welbilt or Dak, the dough will be hard to remove and is best baked right in the machine. After cooling, transfer to a serving dish and brush with the syrup.*

Yield: 1 cake, serving 6 to 8

DOUGH

---

2 teaspoons	active dry yeast
2 cups	bread flour
¼ cup	sugar
½ teaspoon	salt
2 tablespoons	powdered milk
1 tablespoon	grated orange zest
1 stick (½ cup)	unsalted butter
3	eggs
½ cup	water

SYRUP

---

1 cup	sugar
1 cup	water
¼ cup	dark or amber rum (optional)

1. Add all ingredients for the dough in the order suggested by your bread machine manual and process on the dough cycle according to the manufacturer's directions.

2. Preheat the oven to 350 degrees. At the end of the dough cycle, pour the dough from the machine into a greased 2-quart savarin ring mold or a bundt pan. Let rise, lightly covered, 45 minutes in a draftfree place.

3. Bake 30 minutes, until the top is golden. Let cool 15 minutes in the pan.

4. While the cake is cooling, bring the sugar and water for the syrup to a boil, stirring just until the sugar dissolves. Remove from the heat. Add the rum if you wish.

5. Prick the savarin in many places with a toothpick. Brush the warm cake with the hot syrup. Let cool 5 minutes. Invert to unmold the savarin, bottom side-up. Prick what has become the top of the savarin in many places. Brush again with syrup. Continue brushing until all the syrup is used.

6. Serve the savarin plain or fill the center with whipped cream. Or, when it cools, glaze the savarin with melted apricot jam and decorate with sliced almonds and dried apricots or candied fruit.

Tiramisu

Tiramisu *is a sinfully rich dessert made with mascarpone cheese further enriched with either cream or separated eggs and liqueur and cake layers. The bread part is sweet and delicious enough to eat on its own. But don't. It is worth saving for this Italian confection served in some of the world's finest restaurants. Tiramisu freezes wonderfully and can be made a few days ahead, and tastes almost as good right out of the freezer.*

Yield: dessert for 12 from the small loaf, for 20 with the large loaf

SMALL LOAF (1 POUND)	INGREDIENTS	LARGE LOAF (1½ POUNDS)
BREAD		
1½ teaspoons	active dry yeast	2¼ teaspoons
2 cups	bread flour	3 cups
½ teaspoon	salt	¾ teaspoon
⅓ cup	sugar	½ cup
4 tablespoons	unsalted butter, melted and cooled	6 tablespoons
3	egg whites	4
½ cup	water	¾ cup

11 ounces	mascarpone cheese	1 pound (16 ounces)
2 cups	heavy cream	3 cups
1 cup	confectioners' sugar	1½ cups
¼ cup	Amaretto liqueur	⅓ cup
1 tablespoon	vanilla extract	1½ tablespoons
1 cup	strongly brewed espresso	1½ cups
1½ tablespoons	unsweetened cocoa powder	2 tablespoons

1. Add all ingredients for the bread in the order suggested by your bread machine manual and process on the bread cycle according to the manufacturer's directions.
2. When the bread finishes baking, remove from the machine and let cool completely. If possible, make the bread a day ahead so that it will not be too moist. Cut into ½-inch-thick slices. If the bread is very fresh, let the slices dry in a 300 degree oven 10 minutes.
3. By hand or in a mixer, beat the mascarpone until smooth. Beat the cream only until thick. Fold in the mascarpone. Beat in the confectioners' sugar, Amaretto, and vanilla and continue to beat until stiffened to spreading consistency.
4. Dip one side of the bread slices in the espresso. Line the bottom of an 8-by-10-by-2-inch dish for the smaller loaf with the slices set dipped side-up. Use at least a 10-by-12-inch dish for the larger quantity. Spread half of the mascarpone and cream mixture over the bread. Repeat with the second half of the bread and cheese. Sift the cocoa over the top. Cover and refrigerate until serving time or freeze.

Chapter Three
Breads of England, Ireland, Scotland, and Northern Europe

For this chapter, we group Germany, Belgium, Luxembourg, the Netherlands, and Switzerland with the United Kingdom because they are geographically so close together, climatically similar, and great trading partners. England is nearer to Belgium than Los Angeles is to San Francisco. This is Europe untouched by the Mediterranean, centered on the North Sea, often cold and damp.

Except for the most utilitarian sandwich breads, fruits and nuts clutter most loaves. Festive sweet breads full of currants or raisins, almonds or walnuts are common to all of these nations. These trading nations import spices from the East, cocoa beans from Africa, and wheat from Canada for their baking. Dairy farms and orchards at home provide the butter, eggs, apples, oats, and rye.

Few of these breads are light; most are hearty food for the Alps or the Scottish Highlands or coastal villages along the North Sea. Some Britons fry bread for breakfast, but in general, in this part of the world, it is toasted for a morning warmup or to serve with tea. Afternoon tea is responsible for the existence of many wonderful breads and buns that sometimes serve in place of a regular evening meal.

Irish Halloween Bread
(Barmbrack)

Tradition has it that the baker hides a coin in this sweet bread. Some say it will bring good luck, others swear it will bring ghostly visitations.

SMALL LOAF (1 POUND)	INGREDIENTS	LARGE LOAF (1½ POUNDS)
1½ teaspoons	active dry yeast	2¼ teaspoons
2 cups	bread flour	3 cups
2 tablespoons	powdered milk	3 tablespoons
½ teaspoon	salt	¾ teaspoon
½ teaspoon	ground allspice	¾ teaspoon
¼ cup	sugar	⅓ cup
2 tablespoons	grated orange zest	3 tablespoons
2 tablespoons	butter	3 tablespoons
¾ cup plus 2 tablespoons	water	1¼ cups
½ cup	currants	¾ cup
½ cup	golden raisins	¾ cup
1	coin wrapped in foil	1

1. Add all ingredients except the currants, raisins, and coin in the order suggested by your bread machine manual and process on the bread cycle according to the manufacturer's directions.
2. At the beeper (or at the end of the first kneading in the Panasonic, National, and Sanyo), add the currants and raisins and continue on the bread cycle.
3. Grease the outside of the foil-wrapped coin. During the final rising, at least 10 minutes before the bread begins to bake, gently insert the wrapped coin into the center of the loaf so that it is just under the surface. Make sure the lid of the machine is closed and continue the bread cycle.

English White Bread

Here is a wonderful traditional loaf. Slice it thin for watercress or cucumber sandwiches for an English tea. Slice it thick for crisp toast with a soft center or for American-style toasted cheese sandwiches, or better yet, toasted cheese and bacon and tomato sandwiches.

SMALL LOAF (1 POUND)	INGREDIENTS	LARGE LOAF (1½ POUNDS)
1 teaspoon	active dry yeast	1½ teaspoons
2 cups	bread flour	3 cups
2 tablespoons	powdered milk	3 tablespoons
2 tablespoons	sugar	3 tablespoons
2 tablespoons	vegetable oil	3 tablespoons
1 teaspoon	salt	1½ teaspoons
1	whole egg	1
0	egg yolk	1
¾ cup	water	1 cup plus 2 tablespoons

Add all ingredients in the order suggested by your bread machine manual and process on the bread cycle according to the manufacturer's directions.

Sourmilk Oat Bread
(Knaekkebrod)

Cut this high, light, tangy bread into thick slices while it is still warm and eat it right away with a little butter or peanut butter. When cool, if there is any left, slice thin for tuna or egg salad sandwiches.

SMALL LOAF (1 POUND)	INGREDIENTS	LARGE LOAF (1½ POUNDS)
¾ cup plus 2 tablespoons	milk	1¼ cups
1 tablespoon	distilled white vinegar	1½ tablespoons
1½ teaspoons	active dry yeast	2¼ teaspoons
1¾ cups	bread flour	2⅔ cups
½ cup	oatmeal	¾ cup
1½ teaspoons	sugar	2¼ teaspoons
½ teaspoon	salt	¾ teaspoon
2 tablespoons	vegetable oil	3 tablespoons

1. In a cup or small bowl, mix the milk and vinegar. Let stand for about 30 minutes, until the mixture thickens.

2. Add all ingredients including the milk and vinegar in the order suggested by your bread machine manual and process on the bread cycle according to the manufacturer's directions.

Dutch Potato, Onion, and Carrot Bread

In the Netherlands, this vegetable trio turns up together in many dishes, including hutspot, *the national stew. The loaf is filled with vitamins, and it makes dense slices to spread with a slick of sharp mustard and sandwich with ham or lamb.*

SMALL LOAF (1 POUND)	INGREDIENTS	LARGE LOAF (1½ POUNDS)
¼ cup	finely shredded raw potato	⅓ cup
¼ cup	finely shredded raw carrot	⅓ cup
¼ cup	chopped onion	⅓ cup
1½ teaspoons	active dry yeast	2¼ teaspoons
1¾ cups	bread flour	2⅔ cups
½ cup	whole wheat flour	¾ cup
2 tablespoons	wheat germ	3 tablespoons
2 tablespoons	powdered milk	3 tablespoons
1 tablespoon	sugar	1½ tablespoons
½ teaspoon	salt	¾ teaspoon
⅔ cup	water	1 cup

1. Drain the grated potato and carrot well.

2. Add all ingredients in the order suggested by your bread machine manual and process on the bread cycle according to the manufacturer's directions.

Lots of Raisin Bread from Belgium
(Rosynenbrood)

My friend Dede always complains that there are never enough raisins in my breads. "Just hold the raisins together with a little dough," she suggests. That is the Flemish way with this sweet bread that packs raisins to the max.

SMALL LOAF (1 POUND)	INGREDIENTS	LARGE LOAF (1½ POUNDS)
1½ teaspoons	active dry yeast	2¼ teaspoons
2 cups	bread flour	3 cups
2 tablespoons	powdered milk	3 tablespoons
1 teaspoon	salt	1½ teaspoons
1 tablespoon	sugar	1½ tablespoons
¼ cup	vegetable oil	⅓ cup
1	whole egg	1
0	egg yolk	1
⅔ cup	water	1 cup
2 cups	raisins	3 cups

1. Try to use very moist raisins. If they are dried out, place them in a colander, pour about 1 quart of boiling water over them, and let them drain at least 30 minutes.

2. Add all ingredients except the raisins in the order suggested by your bread machine manual and process on the bread cycle according to the manufacturer's directions.

3. At the beeper (or at the end of the first kneading in the Panasonic, Sanyo, and National), add the raisins. Let cool completely before slicing.

Skiers' Bread

When hunger strikes on top of a mountain or tramping through the woods, this is the ideal loaf to find in your backpack. With mashed potatoes, cheese, and fried onions in the bread, the outdoorsman has a hearty sustenance in a few slices. Toasted leftovers make flavorful hors d'oeuvres with wine or beer.

SMALL LOAF (1 POUND)	INGREDIENTS	LARGE LOAF (1½ POUNDS)
1 medium	onion	1 large
1 tablespoon	vegetable oil	1½ tablespoons
1½ teaspoons	active dry yeast	2¼ teaspoons
1½ cups	bread flour	2⅓ cups
¼ cup	wheat bran	¾ cup
1½ teaspoons	sugar	2 teaspoons
½ teaspoon	salt	¾ teaspoon
¾ cup	mashed potatoes	1 cup plus 2 tablespoons
⅔ cup	water	1 cup
¼ cup	shredded Swiss cheese	⅓ cup

1. Coarsely chop the onion. In a medium skillet, sauté in the oil over medium heat until the onion is nicely browned, 15 to 20 minutes. Remove from the heat and let cool to room temperature.

2. Add all ingredients except the onion and cheese in the order suggested by your bread machine manual, adding the mashed potatoes with the water, and process on the bread cycle according to the manufacturer's directions.

3. At the beeper (or at the end of the first kneading in the Panasonic, Sanyo, and National), add the onion and cheese.

Swiss Peasant Bread

This all-purpose, eat-with-anything bread gets its complex and robust flavor from three kinds of flour plus sourdough starter. Even with practically no fat, it stays moist. Any spread, meat, cheese, or pâté is better on this peasant bread.

Yield: 1 (1-pound) loaf

1 teaspoon	active dry yeast
1½ cups	bread flour
½ cup	whole wheat flour
¼ cup	rye flour
1½ teaspoons	sugar
½ teaspoon	salt
1 tablespoon	vegetable oil
½ cup	sourdough starter*
⅔ cup	water

1. Add all ingredients for the dough in the order suggested by your bread machine manual and process on the dough cycle according to the manufacturer's directions.
2. Preheat the oven to 400 degrees. At the end of the dough cycle, remove the dough from the machine. Shape the dough into a large ball, pulling the edges of the dough under and pinching them together to help smooth the top and eliminate air pockets. Cover loosely and let rise in a draftfree place 45 minutes.
3. Dust the top with a little additional flour. With a single-edged razor or a sharp knife, cut a cross on the top of the bread. Place the bread in the oven and reduce the heat to 375 degrees. Bake 40 minutes, or until bread sounds hollow when tapped.

*After measuring out what is needed for this recipe, be sure to replenish your sourdough starter with equal amounts of flour and water.

Saffron Loaf from Cornwall

I have lightened up the real Cornwall buns, once described as "shapeless cakes of dough that are a tribute to the stoicism of the English." Now they are as lively in lemon and mild saffron flavor and light in texture as they are bright yellow in color. You can form them into buns and bake them in the oven or bake as a loaf on the bread cycle as suggested here.

SMALL LOAF (1 POUND)	INGREDIENTS	LARGE LOAF (1½ POUNDS)
1	saffron thread(s)	2
¾ cup	boiling water	1 cup plus 2 tablespoons
1¼ teaspoons	active dry yeast	1¾ teaspoons
2 cups	bread flour	3 cups
½ teaspoon	salt	¾ teaspoon
1 teaspoon	caraway seeds	1½ teaspoons
¼ cup plus 2 tablespoons	sugar	½ cup
1 tablespoon	butter	1½ tablespoons
1	whole egg	1
0	egg white	1
1 tablespoon	candied lemon zest*	1½ tablespoons

1. Add saffron to the boiling water and let cool to room temperature.

2. Add all ingredients including the saffron water in the order suggested by your bread machine manual and process according to the manufacturer's directions.

*See page 169.

Welsh Bread

The play of caraway and raisins here revs up this sweet, light, buttery tea bread. Molasses and brown sugar add almost a butterscotch note. With port wine or coffee after a concert, this is a wonderful way to end an evening. Use your oven broiler or a toaster oven to make outstanding toast.

SMALL LOAF (1 POUND)	INGREDIENTS	LARGE LOAF (1½ POUNDS)
1 teaspoon	distilled white vinegar	1½ teaspoons
⅔ cup	milk	1 cup
1½ teaspoons	active dry yeast	2¼ teaspoons
2 cups	bread flour	3 cups
2 tablespoons	brown sugar	3 tablespoons
½ teaspoon	salt	¾ teaspoon
1 teaspoon	caraway seeds	1½ teaspoons
Pinch	baking soda	⅛ teaspoon
2 tablespoons	molasses	3 tablespoons
4 tablespoons	unsalted butter	6 tablespoons
1	whole egg	1
0	egg white	1
¾ cup	raisins	1 cup

1. Stir the vinegar into the milk. Let stand about 30 minutes, until the mixture thickens.
2. Add all ingredients except the raisins, but including the vinegar and milk, in the order suggested by your bread machine manual and process on the bread cycle according to the manufacturer's directions.
3. At the beeper (or at the end of the first kneading in the Panasonic, Sanyo, and National), add the raisins.

Kaiser Rolls

Yield: 8 rolls

1½ teaspoons	active dry yeast
2 cups	bread flour
2 tablespoons	powdered milk
1 teaspoon	sugar
1 teaspoon	salt
2 teaspoons	barley malt syrup
¾ cup plus 2 tablespoons	water
1 tablespoon	poppy seeds

1. Add all ingredients except the poppy seeds in the order suggested by your bread machine manual and process on the dough cycle according to the manufacturer's directions.

2. Preheat the oven to 450 degrees. When the dough cycle ends, remove the dough from the machine. Divide into 8 pieces. With lightly floured hands, roll each piece into a ball. Press each ball into the poppy seeds. Place with the poppy seed sides up on a lightly greased baking sheet. Leave 2 inches between each roll. Press down to flatten the rolls and help the seeds adhere. With a sharp knife or single-edged razor, score 3 semicircles from the center to the edge of each roll, like spokes on a wheel.

3. Let rise, lightly covered, in a draftfree place 30 minutes, until doubled in size. As soon as the rolls go into the oven, reduce the heat to 375 degrees and bake 15 minutes.

Bratwurst (or Frankfurter) Rolls

These hot dog rolls are good and crusty, full of the flavors of caraway and rye. Since this recipe is made on the dough cycle, it can be prepared ahead and baked just before you cook the sausages or hot dogs.

Yield: 12 rolls

2 teaspoons	active dry yeast
2¼ cups	bread flour
½ cup	rye flour
1 tablespoon	sugar
½ teaspoon	salt
1 tablespoon	caraway seeds
2 tablespoons	vegetable oil
1 cup plus 2 tablespoons	water

1. Add all ingredients in the order suggested by your bread machine manual and process on the dough cycle according to the manufacturer's directions.
2. When the dough cycle ends, remove the dough from the machine. Divide into 12 pieces. On a floured surface, roll each piece into a 6-inch-long stick and place 2 inches apart in a lightly greased baking sheet to rise.
3. Preheat the oven to 375 degrees. Let the rolls rise 20 minutes, or until double in size.
4. Bake 10 to 15 minutes, or until golden brown. Let cool at least 15 minutes. Split the long way.

Crumpets

This is a very liquid batter, which is poured into 3- to 4-inch rings. If you do not have muffin rings, use low 7-ounce cans (the kind tuna comes in) with both the top and bottom lids removed. This recipe will not work in a Welbilt or Dak machine.

Yield: 8 crumpets

2 teaspoons	active dry yeast
1½ cups	bread flour
2 tablespoons	powdered milk
1 teaspoon	sugar
¼ teaspoon	salt
1 tablespoon	vegetable oil
1	whole egg
1 cup	water

1. Add all ingredients for the dough in the order suggested by your bread machine manual and process on the dough cycle according to the manufacturer's directions.
2. At the end of the dough cycle, pour the dough into a pitcher or bowl. Grease 3 or 4 crumpet rings or low 3-inch cans with both ends removed, being sure the top and bottom edges are greased, too.
3. Grease and heat a griddle or heavy frying pan large enough to hold the tins. Place the tins on the griddle or in the pan and pour or ladle ⅓ to ½ cup of dough into each. Cook over medium heat until the tops bubble, about 10 minutes. Remove the rings, turn the crumpets over, and brown on the other side. Repeat until you have used all of the dough. Let cool, then split and toast the crumpets.

Belgian Almond Bread
(Pain d'Amandes Bruxellois)

For dessert or tea, pain d'amandes *is subtly sweet plain or toasted. When it is a day old, cut into thin slices and spread with cream cheese or apricot jam for tea sandwiches. When cut into ½-inch-thick slices and toasted, it reminds me of biscotti.*

SMALL LOAF (1 POUND)	INGREDIENTS	LARGE LOAF (1½ POUNDS)
1½ teaspoons	active dry yeast	2¼ teaspoons
2 cups	bread flour	3 cups
½ teaspoon	ground cinnamon	¾ teaspoon
½ cup	brown sugar	¾ cup
1 teaspoon	salt	1½ teaspoons
4 tablespoons	unsalted butter	6 tablespoons
½ cup	ground almonds	¾ cup
½ teaspoon	almond extract	¾ teaspoon
1 tablespoon	grated orange zest	1½ tablespoons
⅔ cup	water	1 cup

Add all ingredients in the order suggested by your bread machine manual and process on the bread cycle according to the manufacturer's directions.

Bavarian Apple Cake

This sweet, fruit coffee cake makes elderly people, kids, and everyone in between equally happy at a lakeside picnic, as part of an after-concert buffet, or on a winter night around the kitchen table.

Yield: 1 apple cake

DOUGH

1½ teaspoons	active dry yeast
2 cups	bread flour
2 tablespoons	powdered milk
¼ cup	sugar
½ teaspoon	salt
1 tablespoon	grated lemon zest
4 tablespoons	unsalted butter
2	eggs
⅔ cup	water

TOPPING

2	large baking apples
2 tablespoons	sugar
¼ teaspoon	ground cinnamon
⅛ teaspoon	ground cloves

1. Add all ingredients for the dough in the order suggested by your bread machine manual and process on the dough cycle according to the manufacturer's directions.
2. At the end of the dough cycle, remove the dough from the machine. Preheat the oven to 375 degrees.
3. On a lightly greased baking sheet, press out the dough into a 10-inch circle. Peel and core the apples. Cut them into thin slices. Arrange the apple slices in concentric circles on the dough, leaving a ½-inch border around the edge. Mix the sugar with the cinnamon and cloves and sprinkle over the apples. Bake 50 to 60 minutes, until golden brown.

Swiss Dark Chocolate Bread with White Chocolate Chunks

If you bake this bread while your children are out, you might get a chance to enjoy a slice or two. If they are at home, you are out of luck. It is light and not too sweet, perfect with cold milk. The kids might enjoy a dab of peanut butter on top.

SMALL LOAF (1 POUND)	INGREDIENTS	LARGE LOAF (1½ POUNDS)
½ cup	chopped white chocolate or white chocolate chips	¾ cup
1½ teaspoons	active dry yeast	2¼ teaspoons
2 cups	bread flour	3 cups
2 tablespoons	powdered milk	3 tablespoons
¼ cup	unsweetened cocoa powder	⅓ cup
¼ cup	sugar	⅓ cup
4 tablespoons	unsalted butter	6 tablespoons
½ teaspoon	salt	¾ teaspoon
1	whole egg	1
0	egg yolk	1
¾ cup	water	1 cup plus 2 tablespoons

1. Freeze the chopped white chocolate or chips.

2. Add all ingredients except the white chocolate in the order suggested by your bread machine manual and process on the bread cycle according to the manufacturer's directions.

3. At the beeper (or at the end of the first kneading in the National, Sanyo, and Panasonic), add the white chocolate.

Linzer Bread

Traditionally linzer torte has a walnut and cinnamon crust filled with raspberry jam, and it is crisscrossed with more walnut and cinnamon dough. This translates in my recipe into a bread dense with walnuts and perfumed with cinnamon. When it is cool, cut the loaf into thin slices and make small sandwiches filled with raspberry jam to eat with cold milk or hot tea.

SMALL LOAF (1 POUND)	INGREDIENTS	LARGE LOAF (1½ POUNDS)
1½ teaspoons	active dry yeast	2¼ teaspoons
2 cups	bread flour	3 cups
¼ cup	rye flour	⅓ cup
¼ cup	sugar	⅓ cup
½ teaspoon	ground cinnamon	¾ teaspoon
½ teaspoon	salt	¾ teaspoon
½ cup	chopped walnuts	¾ cup
¾ cup plus 2 tablespoons	water	1¼ cups

Add all ingredients in the order suggested by your bread machine manual and process on the bread cycle according to the manufacturer's directions.

German Kuchen

This kuchen, or German coffee cake, is covered with almond streusel, but that can be just a beginning. Substitute other nuts or add dried fruit soaked for half an hour in boiling water. Kuchen is so satisfying that it can become a habit. It is best soon out of the oven for breakfast or tea or for dessert. If you freeze the second kuchen, defrost it in a microwave oven and eat it before it cools completely.

Yield: 2 (9-inch) coffee cakes

DOUGH

1½ teaspoons	active dry yeast
2 cups	bread flour or all-purpose flour
3 tablespoons	sugar
½ teaspoon	salt
4 tablespoons	unsalted butter
1	whole egg
1	egg yolk
¼ teaspoon	ground mace
1 tablespoon	grated lemon zest
⅔ cup	water

1 stick (½ cup)	cold unsalted butter
½ cup	bread flour or all-purpose flour
½ cup	sugar
½ cup	chopped almonds
2 teaspoons	ground cinnamon

1. Add all ingredients for the dough in the order suggested by your bread machine manual and process on the dough cycle according to the manufacturer's directions.
2. Preheat the oven to 350 degrees. To make the streusel, cut the cold butter into pea-sized pieces. In a medium bowl, toss the butter with the other streusel ingredients. The mixture should be very coarse. Cover and refrigerate until ready to use.
3. At the end of the dough cycle, remove the dough from the machine. Divide in half. On a floured surface with a floured rolling pin, roll each piece into a 9-inch circle. Place each round of dough into a lightly greased 9-inch round cake pan. Cover loosely and let rise in a draftfree place about 20 minutes, or until doubled in thickness.
4. Sprinkle half the streusel over each dough round and bake 20 to 25 minutes, or until golden brown. To remove the kuchen from the pan, place a plate on top and invert the pan. Put a serving plate on top and invert again so that the streusel is on top.

Snails
(Schnecken)

Snails, or schnecken, *are German sticky buns that rival muffins and bagels for a quick start in the morning or an afternoon pick-me-up. These do not have honey and are not gooey but a butterscotch and fruit filling is laced throughout the light, gently sweet dough.*

Yield: 12 snails

DOUGH

1½ teaspoons	active dry yeast
2½ cups	bread flour
2 tablespoons	powdered milk
3 tablespoons	sugar
½ teaspoon	salt
2 tablespoons	butter
1	egg
1 cup	buttermilk

FILLING AND TOPPING

¼ cup plus 2 tablespoons	brown sugar
½ teaspoon	ground cinnamon
¼ cup	raisins
1 tablespoon	butter, softened

1. Add all ingredients for the dough in the order suggested by your bread machine manual and process on the dough cycle according to the manufacturer's directions.
2. When the dough cycle ends, remove the dough from the machine. (The dough will be soft.) On a floured board with a floured rolling pin, roll out the dough into an 8-by-16-inch rectangle. Sprinkle ¼ cup of the brown sugar, the cinnamon, and the raisins over the top. From the long side, roll up jelly-roll fashion. Cut into 12 slices.
3. In a 9-by-11-inch nonstick or lightly oiled baking pan, smear the 1 tablespoon butter and sprinkle with the remaining 2 tablespoons brown sugar. Evenly space slices of rolled dough cut side-up on top. Let rise 30 minutes, or until doubled in size.
4. Meanwhile, preheat the oven to 375 degrees. Bake 15 minutes. The dough will run together. Immediately turn out of the pan. Let cool at least 10 minutes before you pull the snails apart.

Chapter Four
Breads of Scandinavia

Denmark, Sweden, Norway, and Finland form their own world of baking, rich with butter and eggs, spiced ryes, and the individual pastries so well known that the whole world calls them by their first name—Danish. These seafaring nations have collected cardamom and cinnamon from the "spice islands" of Indonesia and dried fruits from the Middle East to fill and flavor their breads.

During the long, dark days of a Scandinavian winter, sweet yeast breads help relieve the dreariness. Baking warms the house; a smorgasbord brings people together. In winter or for the long days of summer, open-faced sandwiches, called *smorrebrod*, are made on both dark and light breads seasoned with anise, orange, and cheese. These breads are the forerunners of some of America's best sandwich breads, such as light pumpernickel and caraway rye. The sandwiches are beautifully composed, to my mind sometimes almost too pretty to eat. Tissue slices of meat, fish, cheese, or egg graced with fancifully cut vegetables and rosettes of flavored pastes top the thin slices of firm bread. Both the lightly buttered bread and the toppings must be very fresh and very cleanly cut. And the combinations are endless.

Danish Anise Bread
(Anisbrod)

This big, brown bread is moist and rich, yet light and delicately flavored with anise and almonds. It makes a pot roast sandwich new again, complements vegetable soup or consommé, and goes well with espresso or strong tea.

SMALL LOAF (1 POUND)	INGREDIENTS	LARGE LOAF (1½ POUNDS)
1 teaspoon	active dry yeast	1½ teaspoons
2 cups	bread flour	3 cups
¼ cup	sugar	⅓ cup
½ teaspoon	salt	¾ teaspoon
1 teaspoon	aniseed	1½ teaspoons
¼ cup	toasted almonds, chopped	⅓ cup
2 tablespoons	unsalted butter	3 tablespoons
2 tablespoons	vegetable oil	3 tablespoons
1	whole egg	1
0	egg yolk	1
½ cup	water	¾ cup

Add all ingredients in the order suggested by your bread machine manual and process on the basic bread cycle according to the manufacturer's directions.

Danish Beer Bread
(Ollebrod)

Because it is so assertive, this chewy bread should be sliced thin to go with salty ham or strong cheese. For a traditional Danish open-faced sandwich (smorrebrod), *spread with butter, then top with thinly sliced roast beef and a dollop of prepared horseradish thinned with sour cream.*

SMALL LOAF (1 POUND)	INGREDIENTS	LARGE LOAF (1½ POUNDS)
½ teaspoon	active dry yeast	¾ teaspoon
1¾ cups	bread flour	2⅔ cups
½ cup	rye flour	¾ cup
½ teaspoon	salt	¾ teaspoon
2 tablespoons	molasses	3 tablespoons
½ cup	water	¾ cup
¼ cup	beer	⅓ cup

Add all ingredients in the order suggested by your bread machine manual and process on the basic bread cycle according to the manufacturer's directions.

Scandinavian Black Bread
(Gammelserbrod)

This bread is made in two stages. The sponge is made several hours or a night ahead. Then the rest of the ingredients are added and go through the entire bread cycle. This method produces bread that stays fresh longer and is moist without containing shortening. It is an alternative to the sourdough method. Although it requires planning, the bread machine still does the work. The bread will be slightly sour and dense.

SMALL LOAF (1 POUND)	INGREDIENTS	LARGE LOAF (1½ POUNDS)
1 teaspoon	active dry yeast	1½ teaspoons
½ cup	rye flour	¾ cup
½ cup	water	¾ cup
1½ cups	bread flour	2¼ cups
½ cup	rye flour	¾ cup
½ teaspoon	salt	¾ teaspoon
½ cup	water	¾ cup

1. In a 1-quart bowl, mix the yeast, ½ (¾) cup rye flour, and ½ (¾) cup water. When thoroughly combined, cover loosely and let rise for a few hours or overnight. This is the sponge. The longer it rises, the more sour the bread will be.

2. Add all ingredients in the order suggested by your bread machine manual, adding the sponge with the liquids, and process on the basic bread cycle according to the manufacturer's directions.

Blue Cheese and Walnut Bread

This pungent bread that will appeal to adults makes an excellent hors d'oeuvre with wine, beer, or port. It goes well with a salad or vegetable soup. Leftovers can be cut into small cubes and oven toasted for croutons.

SMALL LOAF (1 POUND)	INGREDIENTS	LARGE LOAF (1½ POUNDS)
1½ teaspoons	active dry yeast	2¼ teaspoons
1½ cups	bread flour	2¼ cups
⅔ cup	rye flour	1 cup
2 tablespoons	powdered milk	3 tablespoons
1½ teaspoons	sugar	2¼ teaspoons
1 teaspoon	salt	1½ teaspoons
1 tablespoon	vegetable oil	1½ tablespoons
¾ cup	water	1 cup plus 2 tablespoons
2 ounces	blue cheese, crumbled	3 ounces
¼ cup	walnuts, coarsely chopped	⅓ cup

1. Add all ingredients except the blue cheese and walnuts in the order suggested by your bread machine manual and process on the bread cycle according to the manufacturer's directions.

2. At the beeper (or at the end of the first kneading in the Panasonic, Sanyo, and National), gradually add the blue cheese and nuts.

Buttermilk Bread with Currants
(Kaernemaelksbrod)

For breakfast or snacking, this bread with its bare hint of sweetness tastes fine on its own. Toasted, it tastes slightly of caramel, yet it is nutritious and very low in fat. This bread is good warm or cold.

SMALL LOAF (1 POUND)	INGREDIENTS	LARGE LOAF (1½ POUNDS)
½ teaspoon	active dry yeast	¾ teaspoon
1¾ cups	bread flour	2⅔ cups
½ cup	whole wheat flour	¾ cup
¼ teaspoon	ground cinnamon	½ teaspoon
2 tablespoons	brown sugar	3 tablespoons
½ teaspoon	salt	¾ teaspoon
1 tablespoon	vegetable oil	1½ tablespoons
1 cup	buttermilk	1½ cups
¼ cup	currants or raisins	⅓ cup

1. Add all ingredients except the currants or raisins in the order suggested by your bread machine manual and process on the variety bread cycle according to the manufacturer's directions.

2. At the beeper (or at the end of the first kneading in the Panasonic, Sanyo, and National), add the currants or raisins.

Danish Caraway Rye Bread
(Kommenbrod)

This loaf is low and dense. Slice it thin. It makes an excellent base for canapés, especially smoked salmon, sardines, and pickled herring. Pass, along with sweet butter, to eat with chowders or barley soups.

SMALL LOAF (1 POUND)	INGREDIENTS	LARGE LOAF (1½ POUNDS)
2 teaspoons	active dry yeast	1 tablespoon
1⅓ cups	bread flour	2 cups
1 cup	rye flour	1½ cups
1 tablespoon	sugar	1½ tablespoons
¾ teaspoon	salt	1 teaspoon
1 teaspoon	caraway seeds	1½ teaspoons
1 tablespoon	vegetable oil	1½ tablespoons
¾ cup plus 2 tablespoons	water	1¼ cups

Add all ingredients in the order suggested by your bread machine manual and process on the basic bread cycle according to the manufacturer's directions.

Swedish Cardamom Bread

For the truest flavor, use cardamom pods rather than ground cardamom. Peel away the outer covering and grind or smash the tiny seeds inside. If pods are not available, ground cardamom will make a less aromatic loaf. A toasted slice is subtly sweet, like biscotti, and just right with coffee. Of course, freshly baked it is at its very best.

SMALL LOAF (1 POUND)	INGREDIENTS	LARGE LOAF (1½ POUNDS)
1 teaspoon	active dry yeast	1¼ teaspoons
2 cups	bread flour	3 cups
½ teaspoon	ground cardamom	¾ teaspoon
2 tablespoons	sugar	3 tablespoons
½ teaspoon	salt	1 teaspoon
2 tablespoons	butter	3 tablespoons
1	whole egg	1
0	egg yolk	1
½ cup	mashed potatoes	¾ cup
½ cup	water	¾ cup
2 tablespoons	sliced almonds	3 tablespoons
2 tablespoons	currants	3 tablespoons

1. Add all ingredients except the almonds and currants in the order suggested by your bread machine manual and process on the bread cycle according to the manufacturer's directions.

2. At the beeper (or at the end of the first kneading in the Panasonic, Sanyo, and National), add the almonds and currants.

Danish Flat Bread
(Fladbrod)

Yield: 4 (10-inch) breads   *Yield: 6 (10-inch) breads*

SMALL LOAF (1 POUND)	INGREDIENTS	LARGE LOAF (1½ POUNDS)
1½ teaspoons	active dry yeast	2¼ teaspoons
1 cup	bread flour	1½ cups
¼ cup	whole wheat flour	⅓ cup
¼ cup	wheat bran	⅓ cup
1 tablespoon	sugar	1½ tablespoons
½ teaspoon	salt	¾ teaspoon
2 tablespoons	butter, melted	3 tablespoons
¼ cup	buttermilk	⅓ cup
½ cup	water	¾ cup

1. Add all ingredients in the order suggested by your bread machine manual and process on the dough cycle according to the manufacturer's directions.
2. At the end of the dough cycle, remove the dough from the machine. Divide into 4 pieces for the small batch or 6 pieces for the large. On a floured board with a floured rolling pin, roll out each piece into a paper-thin circle. While rolling out the dough, heat a large, heavy frying pan, preferably cast iron, until very hot.
3. Do not let the dough rise. Cook each circle in the dry pan over medium heat without turning until the edges are brown. Turn and cook briefly on the other side. These can also be grilled on the barbecue.
4. Let cool before serving. If not eaten right away, store in airtight tins.

Danish Butter Rolls
(Smordejgssnitter)

Yield: 12 rolls

DOUGH

---

2 teaspoons	active dry yeast
2 cups	bread flour
1 tablespoon	sugar
½ teaspoon	salt
5⅓ tablespoons (⅓ cup)	unsalted butter, melted
½ teaspoon	vanilla extract
2	eggs
3 tablespoons	heavy cream
3 tablespoons	water

FILLING

½ cup	chopped walnuts
⅓ cup	sugar

1. Add all ingredients for the dough in the order suggested by your bread machine manual and process on the dough cycle according to the manufacturer's directions.
2. When the dough cycle ends, remove the dough from the machine. Preheat the oven to 400 degrees. Divide the dough into 12 pieces. Roll each piece into a rectangle about 8 inches long. Sprinkle the nuts and sugar over the dough. Roll each piece jelly-roll fashion from the long side and twist into a figure 8.
3. Let rise in a draftfree place 20 minutes, or until doubled in size. Bake 15 minutes, or until golden.

Danish Hazelnut Whole Wheat Bread

This dense, nutty bread tastes good with cream cheese for breakfast, with Danish blue cheese and thin slices of apple for lunch, or with pea soup or roast chicken or ham for dinner. Slice it thin.

SMALL LOAF (1 POUND)	INGREDIENTS	LARGE LOAF (1½ POUNDS)
1½ teaspoons	active dry yeast	2¼ teaspoons
1 cup	bread flour	1½ cups
1 cup	whole wheat flour	1½ cups
2 tablespoons	powdered milk	3 tablespoons
2 tablespoons	brown sugar	3 tablespoons
½ teaspoon	salt	¾ teaspoon
⅓ cup	ground hazelnuts	½ cup
¾ cup plus 2 tablespoons	water	1¼ cups

Add all ingredients in the order suggested by your bread machine manual and process on the basic bread cycle according to the manufacturer's directions.

Danish Sweet Oatmeal and Honey Bread
(Havremelsbrod)

Serve this high, light bread toasted or plain for breakfast. Its mild flavor makes it ideal for sandwiches. Try nut butters, chicken or egg salad, layers of tomatoes, cucumbers, peppers, and sprouts between the slices.

SMALL LOAF (1 POUND)	INGREDIENTS	LARGE LOAF (1½ POUNDS)
1½ teaspoons	active dry yeast	2¼ teaspoons
1¾ cups	bread flour	2⅔ cups
½ cup	oatmeal	¾ cup
2 tablespoons	powdered milk	3 tablespoons
1 teaspoon	salt	1½ teaspoons
2 tablespoons	butter	3 tablespoons
3 tablespoons	honey	¼ cup
1 tablespoon	vegetable oil	1½ tablespoons
¾ cup plus 2 tablespoons	water	1¼ cups
1 tablespoon	butter, melted	1½ tablespoons

1. Add all ingredients except the melted butter in the order suggested by your bread machine manual and process on the bread cycle according to the manufacturer's directions.

2. When you remove the finished bread from the machine, brush the top with the melted butter.

Danish Potato Bread
(Kartoffelbrod)

Potatoes give bread a velvety texture. Leftover mashed potatoes are fine in this recipe. Cold sliced meat and mustard or curried tuna or chicken salad are excellent with potato bread. Serve with highly seasoned stews and soups.

SMALL LOAF (1 POUND)	INGREDIENTS	LARGE LOAF (1½ POUNDS)
1¼ teaspoons	active dry yeast	1¾ teaspoons
2 cups	bread flour	3 cups
2 tablespoons	powdered milk	3 tablespoons
2 tablespoons	sugar	3 tablespoons
½ teaspoon	salt	¾ teaspoon
1	whole egg	1
0	egg yolk	1
2 tablespoons	butter	3 tablespoons
½ cup	mashed potatoes	¾ cup
½ cup	water (If you are boiling potatoes, save the water.)	¾ cup

Add all ingredients in the order suggested by your bread machine manual and process on the bread cycle according to the manufacturer's directions.

Scandinavian Pumpernickel

This moist, tart, full-bodied bread should be sliced thin. For open-faced sandwiches, top with sliced chicken and chutney, roast beef and chopped pickle, or tart apples and havarti or Cheddar cheese. For an hors d'oeuvre, cover with sliced egg and anchovies or smoked fish or cheese.

SMALL LOAF (1 POUND)	INGREDIENTS	LARGE LOAF (1½ POUNDS)
¼ cup	yellow cornmeal	⅓ cup
¾ cup	boiling water	1 cup plus 2 tablespoons
1½ teaspoons	active dry yeast	2¼ teaspoons
1¼ cups	bread flour	2 cups
1 cup	rye flour	1½ cups
1 tablespoon	sugar	1½ tablespoons
½ teaspoon	salt	¾ teaspoon
1 teaspoon	caraway seeds	1½ teaspoons
1 tablespoon	vegetable oil	1½ tablespoons
½ cup	mashed potatoes	¾ cup
¼ cup	water	⅓ cup

1. Place the cornmeal in a small heatproof bowl. Slowly pour the boiling water into the cornmeal, stirring constantly. Let the mixture cool to room temperature.
2. Add all remaining ingredients to your bread machine in the order suggested by your bread machine manual, adding the cornmeal mixture with the liquids, and process on the basic bread cycle according to the manufacturer's directions. Let cool before slicing.

Danish Kringle

This large, buttery coffee or dessert cake is usually made in a pretzel shape or in a circle. The rum is optional, and can be omitted or replaced with orange juice. Kringle makes a delicious, handsome gift.

Yield: 1 large cake

DOUGH

2 teaspoons	active dry yeast
2½ cups	bread flour
2 tablespoons	powdered milk
½ teaspoon	ground cardamom
3 tablespoons	sugar
1 teaspoon	salt
6 tablespoons	unsalted butter
2	egg yolks
¾ cup	water

FILLING AND GLAZE

2 tablespoons	unsalted butter, melted
¼ cup	sugar
1	egg, separated
1½ tablespoons	rum
½ cup	finely chopped almonds

1. Add all ingredients for the dough in the order suggested by your bread machine manual and process on the dough cycle according to the manufacturer's directions.
2. Meanwhile, in a small bowl, whisk together the melted butter and sugar until well blended. Beat in the egg yolk and rum. Add the almonds and mix well.
3. When the dough cycle ends, remove the dough from the machine. On a floured surface, press out the dough into a 12-inch square. Spread the almond filling over the dough and roll up jelly-roll fashion, gently stretching and rolling into a 2-foot-long stick. Set on a nonstick or greased baking sheet and shape into a pretzel or ring. Lightly beat the egg white and brush over dough. Let rise about 25 to 30 minutes, until doubled in size.
4. Meanwhile, preheat the oven to 375 degrees. Bake 20 to 25 minutes, or until golden brown.

Danish Lenten Bread
(Fastelavnsbrod)

Lenten Bread makes a pleasant, light sweet dessert for brunch or a late-night supper. It is especially nice with fresh berries or a syrupy fruit compote.

Yield: 2 (8-inch) rounds

DOUGH

⅔ cup	milk
1 stick (½ cup)	unsalted butter
¼ cup	sugar
1½ teaspoons	active dry yeast
2 cups	bread flour
½ teaspoon	ground cinnamon
¼ teaspoon	salt
1	whole egg
1	egg yolk

TOPPING

1	egg white
2 tablespoons	sugar
¼ cup	chopped almonds

1. In a small saucepan, scald the milk. Add the butter and sugar and let the mixture cool to room temperature. Add all of the ingredients for the dough in the order suggested by your bread machine manual and process on the dough cycle according to the manufacturer's directions.

2. When the dough cycle ends, remove the dough from the machine. Preheat the oven to 350 degrees.

3. Divide the dough into 2 pieces. On a floured surface, roll out each piece into a circle about 8 inches in diameter. Place the circles on a greased baking sheet or sheets. Brush each circle with egg white and sprinkle 1 tablespoon sugar and 2 tablespoons chopped almonds over each circle. Let rise until double in thickness.

4. Bake 20 to 25 minutes, or until golden. Eat warm or cool.

Traditional Danish Pastries

(Sma Smorkager)

Buttery cheese-filled Danish make the best holiday morning treat or night-before-Christmas snack. They can be made a night or a few hours ahead and baked just before eating. Few things smell or taste better than freshly baked Danish.

Yield: 12 cheese Danish

DOUGH

1¼ teaspoons	active dry yeast
2 cups	bread flour
2 tablespoons	powdered milk
3 tablespoons	sugar
½ teaspoon	salt
1 tablespoon	grated lemon zest
1 stick (½ cup)	unsalted butter, cut into small pieces
2	egg yolks
¾ cup	water

FILLING

---

8 ounces	cream cheese, at room temperature
½ cup	sugar
1	whole egg
4 tablespoons	unsalted butter, melted and cooled

---

1. Add all ingredients for the dough in the order suggested by your bread machine manual and process on the dough cycle according to the manufacturer's directions.
2. At the end of the dough cycle, remove the dough from the machine. Refrigerate on a greased plate while you make the filling, or refrigerate in a covered bowl overnight.
3. In a medium bowl, mix all ingredients for the filling until smooth.
4. With a floured rolling pin on a floured surface, roll out the dough into a 12-by-16-inch rectangle. Cut into 12 (4-inch) squares. Spoon 2 tablespoons of filling onto each square. Pinch together 2 opposite corners of each square. Pinch together the other pair of corners, making each square into a sealed package. Place the Danish pastries 2 inches apart on a greased baking sheet.
5. Preheat the oven to 350 degrees. Allow the Danish to rise 30 minutes, or until puffy. Bake 15 minutes, until golden.

Low-Fat Danish

If you love morning sweet breads, but cannot afford the cholesterol, this healthier version of Danish pastry will make you happy. Substitute jam for the filling if you do not like prunes.

Yield: 12 (4-inch) Danish

DOUGH

2 teaspoons	active dry yeast
2½ cups	bread flour
2 tablespoons	powdered milk
¼ cup	sugar
½ teaspoon	salt
1 teaspoon	vanilla extract
1	whole egg
¾ cup	water

FILLING AND GLAZE

½ cup	water
1 cup	pitted prunes
½ teaspoon	ground cinnamon
¼ cup	ground or finely chopped almonds
1	egg white

1. Add all ingredients for the dough in the order suggested by your bread machine manual and process on the dough cycle according to the manufacturer's directions.
2. At the end of the dough cycle, remove the dough from the machine. Refrigerate on a greased plate while you make the filling.
3. In a small saucepan, bring the ½ cup water for the filling to a boil. Add the prunes and boil 3 to 5 minutes, until most of the water evaporates and the prunes are plumped; drain off any excess liquid. Chop the prunes and add the prunes and cinnamon to the almonds. Mix well.
4. On a floured surface, press or roll out the dough to a 12-by-16-inch rectangle. Cut into 12 (4-inch) squares. Spoon about 1½ tablespoons of filling into the center of each square. Press together 2 opposite corners of each square. Press together the other pair of corners to form a sealed package. Place the Danish pastries 2 inches apart on a greased baking sheet.
5. Preheat the oven to 350 degrees. Brush the beaten egg white over the pastry. Let the Danish rise 30 minutes, or until puffy. Bake 15 minutes, or until golden.

Danish Shrovetide Buns
(Fastelavnsboller)

This fried pastry is close to the New Orleans beignet—a doughnut without a hole, best eaten hot. Making and eating Shrovetide buns is a cheerful way to spend a rainy day at a vacation house. They are the friendliest and least expensive party food.

Yield: 16 buns

1½ teaspoons	active dry yeast
½ cup	mashed potatoes
¾ cup	water (save the water from cooking the potatoes)
3½ cups	bread flour
1 tablespoon	vegetable oil
⅓ cup	sugar
½ teaspoon	salt
2 cups	vegetable oil, for frying
2 tablespoons	confectioners' sugar

1. In a large bowl, mix the yeast, mashed potatoes, water, and 1 cup of the bread flour. Cover and let stand 2 hours at room temperature or overnight in the refrigerator.

2. Add the potato mixture and all other ingredients except the oil and confectioners' sugar in the order suggested by your bread machine manual and process on the dough cycle according to the manufacturer's directions.

3. At the end of the dough cycle, remove the dough from the machine. The dough can be refrigerated for a few hours at this point.

4. On a floured surface, roll out the dough about ½ inch thick. Cut into 2-inch squares or rounds.

5. In a large saucepan or deep skillet, heat at least 1 inch of oil until a small piece of dough sizzles immediately on contact. Fry 3 or 4 buns at a time 10 to 15 seconds, until golden. Turn and fry on the other side until lightly browned. Drain on crumpled brown paper bags or on several layers of newspapers covered with a sheet of paper towel.

6. Sprinkle with confectioners' sugar.

Swedish Rye

Roast beef or pot roast with horseradish dressing, baked ham, tuna salad, or sliced crisp vegetables make lively sandwiches on this dense, spiced bread. Let cool completely before cutting into thin slices. This is a fine base for open-faced sandwiches and canapés of smoked fish or assertive cheese.

SMALL LOAF (1 POUND)	INGREDIENTS	LARGE LOAF (1½ POUNDS)
1½ teaspoons	active dry yeast	2¼ teaspoons
1½ cups	bread flour	2¼ cups
¾ cup	rye flour	1 cup plus 2 tablespoons
2 tablespoons	powdered milk	3 tablespoons
½ teaspoon	salt	¾ teaspoon
2 teaspoons	sugar	1 tablespoon
1 teaspoon	aniseed	1½ teaspoons
1 teaspoon	grated orange zest	1½ teaspoons
1 tablespoon	vegetable oil	1½ tablespoons
¼ cup	dark corn syrup	⅓ cup
¾ cup plus 2 tablespoons	water	1¼ cups

Add all ingredients in the order suggested by your bread machine manual and process on the bread cycle according to the manufacturer's directions.

Chapter Five
Breads of Africa

Breads are the center of the meal in much of Africa. In East Africa, flat breads serve as utensils for gathering up the food, acting as both plate and fork. Maize and millet, nuts and fiery peppers, sweet potatoes and bananas contribute to distinctive breads. In many of these countries, bread is the daily staple, often with a little meat or vegetables to accompany it. Of course, on holidays, whether a Christian or Muslim celebration, bread remains an important part of the feast.

For nomads, who trekked across the African deserts or through the deep forests and open velds, bread has always been the easiest food for travel, nothing to leak or spoil quickly, easy to bake over an open fire.

To turn some traditional recipes into bread machine loaves, I have added yeast to breads that were dry, dense, and originally cooked in an iron pan or on a stone. I have lightened some, but most are still assertive, not just filling supporting roles in a meal.

East African Chickpea and Green Olive Bread

Traditionally, this dough is rolled, cut into a fish shape, and baked for a Lenten treat. But it tastes wonderful made on the bread cycle of the machine. Grill ½-inch-thick slices and dip into clarified Ethiopian spiced butter (page 133). Serve with beer, dry wine, iced tea, or lemonade for an hors d'oeuvre or with roast lamb for dinner.

SMALL LOAF (1 POUND)	INGREDIENTS	LARGE LOAF (1½ POUNDS)
1½ teaspoons	active dry yeast	2¼ teaspoons
1½ cups	bread flour	2¼ cups
¾ cup	chickpea flour*	1 cup plus 2 tablespoons
½ teaspoon	salt	¾ teaspoon
⅛ teaspoon	ground black pepper or crushed hot red pepper	¼ teaspoon
½ cup	chopped onions	¾ cup
1	garlic clove(s), minced	1½
2 tablespoons	vegetable oil	3 tablespoons
¼ cup	chopped green olives	⅓ cup
½ cup	water	¾ cup

Add all ingredients in the order suggested by your bread machine manual and process on the bread cycle according to the manufacturer's directions.

Ethiopian Spiced Butter

Bring 1 pound of unsalted butter to a boil. Add a small onion, chopped; 2 teaspoons grated ginger; 1 tablespoon minced garlic; 2 whole cloves; ¼ teaspoon cardamom seeds; 1 teaspoon ground turmeric; 1 cinnamon stick; and ⅛ teaspoon nutmeg. Cook over low heat 45 minutes without stirring. Strain and save the clear clarified spiced butter; discard the solids at the bottom of the pan.

*Chickpea flour is available at health food stores and Indian groceries. Or see mail-order sources on page 10.

Ethiopian Spiced Flat Bread
(Yewollo Dabo)

While this bread functions as a daily staple in Africa, in the United States it can be eaten as an hors d'oeuvre. Heavily spiced, it tastes fine with beer, ginger ale, and tea. Cut or tear the bread to eat plain or with chickpea or sour cream dips.

Yield: 1 (10- to 12-inch) flat bread

DOUGH	
1¼ teaspoons	active dry yeast
1¼ cups	bread flour
1 cup	whole wheat flour
⅛ teaspoon	ground cinnamon
¼ teaspoon	ground black pepper
Pinch	ground cloves
1 teaspoon	ground coriander
1 teaspoon	ground cardamom
1 teaspoon	salt
1 teaspoon	sugar
1 cup	water

TOPPING	
1 tablespoon	butter, at room temperature
1 teaspoon	Berber spice mixture*

1. Add all ingredients for the dough in the order suggested by your bread machine manual and process on the dough cycle according to the manufacturer's directions.
2. At the end of the dough cycle, remove the dough from the machine. Preheat the oven to 350 degrees.
3. On a lightly greased baking sheet, with floured fingers, press the dough into a 10- to 12-inch circle. Let rise 25 minutes. Bake 50 minutes, or until golden.
4. Mix butter and Berber spice mixture and spread sparingly on hot flat bread. Serve warm. Tear apart with your hands; do not cut.

*If you cannot find this hot African spice mixture, make it by grinding together equal amounts of ground ginger, black pepper, cardamom, cumin, and cayenne.

Ethiopian Millet Bread
(Injera)

In Ethiopia, injera, *a flat, almost cloth-like bread, serves as a utensil for picking up food or mopping up tasty sauces. This version is higher and lighter, yet perfect for soaking up the last spicy gravy. Slice ½ inch thick for crisp, yellow toast and use under piquantly sauced poached or fried eggs.*

SMALL LOAF (1 POUND)	INGREDIENTS	LARGE LOAF (1½ POUNDS)
½ cup	millet meal*	¾ cup
½ cup	boiling water	¾ cup
1½ teaspoons	active dry yeast	2¼ teaspoons
1½ cups	bread flour	2¼ cups
¼ teaspoon	ground turmeric	½ teaspoon
1 teaspoon	salt	1½ teaspoons
1 tablespoon	vegetable oil	1½ tablespoons
½ cup	water	¾ cup

1. Add the millet to the boiling water, stirring until smooth. Remove from the heat and let cool to room temperature.

2. Add all ingredients in the order suggested by your bread machine manual, adding the millet along with the liquids. Process according to the manufacturer's directions.

*Millet meal is available at health food stores. Or see mail-order sources on page 10.

East African Banana and Coconut Bread

The fruit and fiber content alone justifies eating this sweet, slightly sticky bread even for breakfast. Toasting intensifies the coconut and banana flavors. No butter or jam needed, even for an afternoon pick-me-up with tea.

SMALL LOAF (1 POUND)	INGREDIENTS	LARGE LOAF (1½ POUNDS)
1½ teaspoons	active dry yeast	2¼ teaspoons
1¾ cups	bread flour	2⅔ cups
½ cup	whole wheat flour	¾ cup
2 tablespoons	wheat bran	3 tablespoons
2 tablespoons	sugar	3 tablespoons
1 teaspoon	salt	1½ teaspoons
½ cup	mashed ripe banana	¾ cup
½ cup	unsweetened coconut milk	¾ cup
¼ cup	water	⅓ cup
½ cup	flaked coconut	¾ cup
½ cup	raisins	¾ cup

1. Add all ingredients except the shredded coconut and raisins in the order suggested by your bread machine manual and process on the bread cycle according to the manufacturer's directions.

2. At the beeper (or at the end of the first kneading in the Panasonic, Sanyo, and National), add the coconut and raisins.

East African Peanut and Chili Bread

This bread borrows the spicy, nutty flavor of a traditional East African soup and mellows it into a snappy sandwich bread that is perfect for cold roast meats and chicken or for a light cucumber sandwich.

SMALL LOAF (1 POUND)	INGREDIENTS	LARGE LOAF (1½ POUNDS)
1½ teaspoons	active dry yeast	2¼ teaspoons
2 tablespoons	wheat germ	3 tablespoons
2 cups	bread flour	3 cups
2 tablespoons	powdered milk	3 tablespoons
¼ teaspoon	cayenne or ground hot red pepper	½ teaspoon
½ teaspoon	salt	¾ teaspoon
1 tablespoon	sugar	1½ tablespoons
1	garlic clove(s), minced	1½
¾ cup plus 2 tablespoons	water	1¼ cups
¼ cup	creamy peanut butter	⅓ cup

Add all ingredients in the order suggested by your bread machine manual and process on the bread cycle according to the manufacturer's directions.

South African Sweet Potato Bread

This gingery, orange-scented bread turns into a wonderful chicken salad or nutted cheese sandwich. It is lovely sliced thin and oven toasted with a dab of cottage cheese or crème fraîche. Make leftovers into croutons to serve with curry or on fruit salad.

SMALL LOAF (1 POUND)	INGREDIENTS	LARGE LOAF (1½ POUNDS)
½ cup	mashed cooked sweet potato	¾ cup
⅓ cup	water	½ cup
1½ teaspoons	active dry yeast	2¼ teaspoons
2 cups	bread flour	3 cups
2 tablespoons	wheat bran	3 tablespoons
2 tablespoons	brown sugar	3 tablespoons
1 tablespoon	candied orange zest*	1½ tablespoons
1 teaspoon	salt	1½ teaspoons
1 teaspoon	ground ginger	1½ teaspoons
1 teaspoon	curry powder	1½ teaspoons
2	egg whites	3
¼ cup	coarsely chopped peanuts	⅓ cup

1. Blend the sweet potato and water.
2. Add all ingredients except the peanuts in the order suggested by your bread machine manual and process on the bread cycle according to the manufacturer's directions.
3. At the beeper (or at the end of the first kneading in the Panasonic, Sanyo, and National), add the peanuts.

*See page 169.

South African Toasted Coconut
and Lemon Bread

Candied lemon zest and coconut—a flavor combination derived from a popular South African pie—rev up this very proper tea bread. Ice cream or tropical fruit, such as mango, can turn slices into a lovely dessert.

SMALL LOAF (1 POUND)	INGREDIENTS	LARGE LOAF (1½ POUNDS)
½ cup	flaked coconut	¾ cup
1½ teaspoons	active dry yeast	2¼ teaspoons
2 cups	bread flour	3 cups
2 tablespoons	sugar	3 tablespoons
1 teaspoon	salt	1½ teaspoons
1 tablespoon	vegetable oil	1½ tablespoons
2 tablespoons	candied lemon zest*	3 tablespoons
¾ cup plus 2 tablespoons	water	1¼ cups

1. Preheat the oven to 350 degrees. Spread the coconut on a baking sheet and bake 10 minutes, until toasted and lightly browned. Remove to a plate and let cool.
2. Add all ingredients in the order suggested by your bread machine manual and process on the bread cycle according to the manufacturer's directions.

*See page 169.

Fresh Corn Bread from Central Africa

"Green mealie" is an African pudding made from corn. I have veered from tradition by transforming it into a yeast bread. In summer, use leftover fresh corn. In winter, frozen or canned corn will do. Serve with gazpacho or broiled fish.

SMALL LOAF (1 POUND)	INGREDIENTS	LARGE LOAF (1½ POUNDS)
1½ teaspoons	active dry yeast	2¼ teaspoons
2 cups	bread flour	3 cups
2 tablespoons	powdered milk	3 tablespoons
1 teaspoon	salt	1½ teaspoons
2 tablespoons	sugar	3 tablespoons
1 tablespoon	butter	1½ tablespoons
⅔ cup	corn kernels—cooked, frozen, or canned	1 cup
½ cup	water	¾ cup

Add all ingredients in the order suggested by your bread machine manual and process on the bread cycle according to the manufacturer's directions. Let cool before slicing.

Moroccan Almond and Prune Bread

Cream cheese, yogurt cheese, or crème fraîche between slices of this dark, fruity bread make an exceptional tea sandwich. For an open-faced sandwich, top with cold chicken and chutney.

SMALL LOAF (1 POUND)	INGREDIENTS	LARGE LOAF (1½ POUNDS)
⅓ cup	pitted prunes	½ cup
⅔ cup	boiling water	1 cup
1½ teaspoons	active dry yeast	2¼ teaspoons
1¾ cups	bread flour	2⅔ cups
⅓ cup	whole wheat flour	½ cup
2 tablespoons	wheat germ	3 tablespoons
2 tablespoons	sugar	3 tablespoons
1 teaspoon	ground cinnamon	1½ teaspoons
1 tablespoon	grated orange zest	1½ tablespoons
½ teaspoon	salt	¾ teaspoon
½ cup	sliced or coarsely chopped almonds	¾ cup

1. Chop the prunes and add to the boiling water. Let cool to room temperature.
2. Add all ingredients except the almonds, but including the prunes with their soaking liquid, in the order suggested by your bread machine manual and process on the bread cycle according to the manufacturer's directions.
3. At the beeper (or at the end of the first kneading in the Panasonic, Sanyo, and National), add the almonds.

Ethiopian Honey Bread
(Yemarina Yewolet Dabo)

This aromatic bread, sweetly spiced with ground coriander, cinnamon and cloves, is lovely spread with butter and perhaps just a drizzle of honey. Serve with tea or lemonade or with fruit salad. For a sandwich, fill with mild cheese or sliced turkey.

SMALL LOAF (1 POUND)	INGREDIENTS	LARGE LOAF (1½ POUNDS)
⅔ cup	milk	1 cup
2 tablespoons	butter	3 tablespoons
¼ cup	honey	⅓ cup
1¼ teaspoons	active dry yeast	2 teaspoons
1¾ cups	bread flour	2⅔ cups
½ cup	whole wheat flour	¾ cup
½ teaspoon	ground coriander	¾ teaspoon
¼ teaspoon	ground cinnamon	½ teaspoon
¼ teaspoon	ground cloves	½ teaspoon
1 teaspoon	salt	1½ teaspoons
1	whole egg	1
0	egg yolk	1

1. In a small saucepan, heat the milk just until it foams around the edges. Remove from the heat. Add the butter and honey and stir until melted. Let cool to room temperature.

2. Add all ingredients in the order suggested by your bread machine manual and process on the bread cycle according to the manufacturer's directions.

West African Banana Fritters

These fritters, similar to what we know as beignets, make inexpensive party food rich in natural fruit flavors. Children will enjoy munching these crispies with milk, but the big kids will eat their way through an endless supply with coffee or beer.

Yield: 24 fritters

DOUGH	
2 teaspoons	active dry yeast
1¾ cups	bread flour
½ cup	whole wheat flour
2 tablespoons	sugar
½ teaspoon	salt
½ cup	flaked coconut
1 cup	mashed ripe banana
1	egg
¼ cup	milk

FRYING AND TOPPING	
2 to 4 cups	vegetable oil, for frying
½ cup	confectioners' sugar

1. Add all ingredients for the dough in the order suggested by your bread machine manual and process on the dough cycle according to the manufacturer's directions.
2. When the dough cycle ends, remove the dough from the machine. On a floured surface with a floured rolling pin, roll out the dough into an 8-by-12-inch rectangle. Cut into 2-inch squares. Place on a nonstick or greased tray, cover, and let rise in a draftfree place about 30 minutes.
3. In a large saucepan or skillet, heat at least 1 inch of oil to 365 degrees on a deep-frying thermometer. Fry 3 or 4 fritters at a time 10 to 15 seconds on one side until golden. Turn carefully and fry the other side until lightly browned, 5 to 7 seconds. Drain quickly on crumpled brown paper bags or on several layers of newspaper covered with a sheet of paper towel.
4. Sprinkle with confectioners' sugar. Eat while still warm.

South African Braided Crullers
(Koeksusters)

These sweet breads are as good looking as they are time consuming, but fun to make. On a rainy day when the children are out of school, braiding koeksusters *(sometimes spelled* koesisters*) will keep them busy and happy.*

Yield: 24 crullers

DOUGH

2 teaspoons	active dry yeast
2 cups	bread flour
½ teaspoon	ground cinnamon
½ teaspoon	grated nutmeg
½ teaspoon	salt
2 tablespoons	butter or lard
¾ cup	buttermilk

SYRUP AND FRYING

1 cup	sugar
½ cup	water
1	cinnamon stick
1	strip of lemon peel
Pinch	cream of tartar
Pinch	salt
2 to 4 cups	vegetable oil, for frying

---

1. Add all ingredients for the dough in the order suggested by your bread machine manual and process on the dough cycle according to the manufacturer's directions.
2. When the dough cycle ends, remove the dough from the machine. On a floured surface with a floured rolling pin, roll out the dough into a 8-by-12-inch rectangle about ¼ inch thick. Cut into 24 strips, each 4 by 1 inch.
3. Hold each strip the long way. Cut 2 parallel lines ¾ of the way up the strip so that you have 3 pieces still attached across the top inch to braid. Braid each cruller loosely. Pinch and tuck the end of each under. Place the braids 1 inch apart on a lightly greased baking sheet. Cover loosely and let rise in a draftfree place 20 minutes.
4. While the crullers are rising, make the syrup: In a medium saucepan, heat the sugar, water, cinnamon stick, lemon peel, cream of tartar, and salt until all of the sugar dissolves and the liquid is clear. Strain and discard the lemon and cinnamon. Let the syrup cool.
5. In a wok or large saucepan, heat at least 1 inch of oil to 365 degrees. Fry 3 or 4 crullers at a time 20 to 30 seconds on one side, until golden. Turn carefully and fry the other side until lightly browned, about 20 seconds longer. Drain quickly on crumpled brown paper bags or on several layers of newspaper covered with a sheet of paper towel.
6. Place the hot crullers in the cool syrup. Eat immediately.

Chapter Six

Breads of the Caribbean and Latin America

With immigrants to the New World from Africa, Spain, and India came curries and coconut milk, garlic and onions to add to the indigenous corn and chilies, fabulous fruits, spices, and quinoa and amaranth grains native to Latin America and the Caribbean. Most of the world's sugarcane grows here; cinnamon, nutmeg, coconut, and mangoes grow on trees. Pineapple is so sweet. Every island and nation from northern Mexico to southern Chile has its special sweet bread.

In this part of the world, where sandwiches are not so common, yeast breads are usually served for breakfast or dessert. With meat or fish one eats starchy potato, *akee*, or cassava, not bread. Bread is to savor on its own with only coffee or a cool drink. An exception is the plain Cuban Bread, which is often filled with roast pork to make a savory Cuban sandwich. Today every ethnic group in Trinidad makes a version of Indian *dalpuri*, which was brought by the indentured laborers shipped by the British from India to work in the sugarcane fields more than a century ago. In Argentina,

Spanish garlic and parsley go with everything. In Bermuda, sweet breads are heavy, laden with British currants and candied fruits.

The United States is not the only melting-pot culture. Our neighbors to the south are derived from an intriguing mixture of cultures that once seemed foreign to us. Now Latin American and Caribbean immigrants to the United States are bringing their *bakes* and *empanadas* with them, turning what was formerly exotic into familiar home cooking.

Amaranth and Orange Bread

Although it has no nuts, this bread is nutty and fruity, dense and healthy. Amaranth, a high-protein grain from Central America, contributes the mellow flavor that goes so well with orange and honey. It is wonderful to wake up to the smell of amaranth bread and to start the day with a wallop of taste and nutrition.

SMALL LOAF (1 POUND)	INGREDIENTS	LARGE LOAF (1½ POUNDS)
1½ teaspoons	active dry yeast	2¼ teaspoons
1⅔ cups	bread flour	2½ cups
¼ cup	whole wheat flour	⅓ cup
½ cup	amaranth flour*	¾ cup
2 tablespoons	powdered milk	3 tablespoons
2 tablespoons	honey	3 tablespoons
2 tablespoons	grated orange zest	3 tablespoons
½ teaspoon	salt	¾ teaspoon
1 tablespoon	vegetable oil	1½ tablespoons
¾ cup plus 2 tablespoons	water	1¼ cups

Add all ingredients in the order suggested by your bread machine manual and process on the bread cycle according to the manufacturer's directions.

*Available at health food stores.

Argentine Chimichurri Bread

This soft, full-flavored bread generously mops up the juices of roast beef, pork, or chicken at dinner. At lunch, this is the best choice for a grilled steak or cold lamb or turkey sandwich, since it takes its flavor from chimichurri, *the traditional Argentine sauce for meat. Definitely skip this bread at breakfast.*

SMALL LOAF (1 POUND)	INGREDIENTS	LARGE LOAF (1½ POUNDS)
1¼ teaspoons	active dry yeast	1¾ teaspoons
2 cups	bread flour	3 cups
2 tablespoons	wheat bran	3 tablespoons
2 teaspoons	sugar	1 tablespoon
1 teaspoon	salt	1½ teaspoons
2 tablespoons	chopped parsley	3 tablespoons
2 tablespoons	chopped onion	3 tablespoons
1	garlic clove(s), minced	1½
½ teaspoon	dried oregano	¾ teaspoon
Pinch	cayenne pepper	⅛ teaspoon
2 tablespoons	olive oil	3 tablespoons
1 tablespoon	white wine vinegar	1½ tablespoons
¾ cup	water	1 cup

Add all ingredients in the order suggested by your bread machine manual and process on the bread cycle according to the manufacturer's directions.

Argentine Cheese and Corn Bread

Similar breads appear all over South America as far north as Venezuela. This version from the southern tip of the continent has enough color and taste to be eaten plain or with a meat broth or boiled beef.

SMALL LOAF (1 POUND)	INGREDIENTS	LARGE LOAF (1½ POUNDS)
1½ teaspoons	active dry yeast	2¼ teaspoons
1½ cups	bread flour	2¼ cups
1 cup	yellow cornmeal	1½ cups
2 teaspoons	sugar	1 tablespoon
½ teaspoon	salt	¾ teaspoon
2 tablespoons	grated Parmesan cheese	3 tablespoons
⅛ teaspoon	ground black pepper	¼ teaspoon
1 teaspoon	ground cumin	1½ teaspoons
2 tablespoons	vegetable oil	3 tablespoons
⅔ cup	water	1 cup
¼ cup	finely diced green bell pepper	⅓ cup
¼ cup	corn kernels	⅓ cup

1. Add all ingredients except the bell pepper and corn in the order suggested by your bread machine manual and process on the bread cycle according to the manufacturer's directions.

2. At the beeper (or at the end of the first kneading in the Panasonic, National, and Sanyo), add the bell pepper and corn.

Trinidad Coconut Bread
(Bakes)

This recipe for bakes comes from Trinidadian Maureen Mathura, whose family eats bakes for breakfast. "It is a cross between bread and cake," she says. Early morning, before the heat of the day, commercial bakers as well as home cooks make mildly sweet, coconut bakes in Trinidad and Tobago.

SMALL LOAF (1 POUND)	INGREDIENTS	LARGE LOAF (1½ POUNDS)
1½ teaspoons	active dry yeast	2¼ teaspoons
2 cups	bread flour	3 cups
¼ teaspoon	baking soda	½ teaspoon
½ cup	flaked coconut	¾ cup
1 teaspoon	salt	1½ teaspoons
2 tablespoons	sugar	3 tablespoons
2 tablespoons	butter	3 tablespoons
½ cup	unsweetened coconut milk	¾ cup
½ cup	water	¾ cup

Add all ingredients in the order suggested by your bread machine manual and process on the bread cycle according to the manufacturer's directions.

Sweet Caribbean Corn Bread
(Pan Dulce de Harina de Maiz)

The crunch of cornmeal adds another dimension to this light, slightly sweet, clove-scented bread. Raisins and lemon zest make it even more lively. For a sandwich, fill with mild cheese or sliced chicken. Thin slices make a casual hors d'oeuvre with rum punch or lemonade.

SMALL LOAF (1 POUND)	INGREDIENTS	LARGE LOAF (1½ POUNDS)
1½ teaspoons	active dry yeast	2¼ teaspoons
1¾ cups	flour	2⅔ cups
⅓ cup	yellow cornmeal	½ cup
2 tablespoons	sugar	3 tablespoons
1 teaspoon	salt	1½ teaspoons
¼ teaspoon	ground cloves	¼ teaspoon
2 tablespoons	candied lemon zest*	3 tablespoons
½ cup	unsweetened coconut milk	¾ cup
½ cup	water	¾ cup
½ cup	raisins	¾ cup

1. Add all ingredients except the raisins in the order suggested by your bread machine manual and process on the bread cycle according to the manufacturer's directions.

2. At the beeper (or at the end of the first kneading in the Panasonic, Sanyo, and National), add the raisins.

*See page 169.

Corn and Black Olive Bread

In Peru, this piquant corn bread (usually made without yeast) plus potatoes makes a meal. With baked or grilled fish, it becomes a banquet. Toast and top with guacamole or meat loaf or Cheddar cheese.

SMALL LOAF (1 POUND)	INGREDIENTS	LARGE LOAF (1½ POUNDS)
1½ teaspoons	active dry yeast	2¼ teaspoons
1¾ cups	bread flour	2⅔ cups
⅓ cup	yellow cornmeal	½ cup
½ cup	corn kernels (raw or frozen and thawed)	¾ cup
¼ cup	chopped black olives	⅓ cup
2 tablespoons	grated Parmesan or Romano cheese	3 tablespoons
½ teaspoon	ground black pepper	¾ teaspoon
1	garlic clove(s), minced	1½
½ teaspoon	salt	¾ teaspoon
½ cup	water	¾ cup
¼ cup	chopped walnuts	⅓ cup

1. Add all ingredients except the walnuts according to your bread machine manual and process on the bread cycle according to the manufacturer's directions.
2. At the beeper (or at the end of the first kneading in the Panasonic, National, and Sanyo), add the walnuts.

Cuban Bread

This simple, thick-crusted bread was brought to the United States by Cuban emigrés in the 1960s and popularized in the Cuban sandwich filled with ham or roast pork, onion, and tomato. The sandwich is pressed down and grilled in Cuban restaurants both plain and fancy in Miami and Manhattan.

Yield: 2 loaves

1½ teaspoons	active dry yeast
2 cups	bread flour
1 teaspoon	sugar
1 tablespoon	olive oil
½ teaspoon	salt
¾ cup plus 2 tablespoons	water

1. Add all ingredients in the order suggested by your bread machine manual and process on the dough cycle according to the manufacturer's directions.

2. *Do not preheat the oven.* When the dough cycle ends, remove the dough from the machine and divide in half. Roll each piece into a 12-inch log. Place 2 inches apart on a lightly greased baking sheet. With a sharp knife or single-edged razor blade, cut 3 parallel diagonal slits in the top of each loaf. *Do not let rise.*

3. Place in the cold oven. Turn the heat to 375 degrees. Bake 30 minutes, or until the loaf sounds hollow when the bottom is tapped.

Colombian Potato and Cheese Bread

This moist, fragrant bread won the fast bread contest: It was eaten faster than all other breads. It is so satisfying that fillings and spreads are not needed. Cut the loaf into ½-inch slices and then into triangles for hors d'oeuvres with beer, sangria, or orange juice lightened with club soda.

SMALL LOAF (1 POUND)	INGREDIENTS	LARGE LOAF (1½ POUNDS)
1½ teaspoons	active dry yeast	2¼ teaspoons
2 cups	bread flour	3 cups
½ cup	mashed potatoes	¾ cup
½ cup	chopped onion	¾ cup
2 tablespoons	grated Parmesan cheese	3 tablespoons
1 tablespoon	chopped cilantro or parsley	1½ tablespoons
1 teaspoon	ground cumin	1½ teaspoons
1 teaspoon	dried oregano	1½ teaspoons
1 teaspoon	salt	1½ teaspoons
⅓ cup	water	½ cup
¼ cup	chopped and drained tomato	⅓ cup

1. Add all ingredients except the tomato in the order suggested by your bread machine manual and process on the bread cycle according to the manufacturer's directions.

2. At the beeper (or at the end of the first kneading in the Panasonic, National, and Sanyo), add the tomato.

Puerto Rican Pan de Mallorca

In Puerto Rico, this bread is usually baked in a ring, sliced, and spread generously with butter. The bread machine yields a light, almost fluffy loaf, which toasts well in ½-inch-thick slices and makes lovely thin cucumber sandwiches for tea when a day old.

SMALL LOAF (1 POUND)	INGREDIENTS	LARGE LOAF (1½ POUNDS)
1¼ teaspoons	active dry yeast	1¾ teaspoons
2 cups	bread flour	3 cups
1 tablespoon	sugar	1½ tablespoons
1 teaspoon	salt	1½ teaspoons
1 tablespoon	olive oil	1½ tablespoons
1	whole egg	1
0	egg yolk	1
⅓ cup	sourdough starter*	½ cup
⅔ cup	water	1 cup

Add all ingredients in the order suggested by your bread machine manual and process on the bread cycle according to the manufacturer's directions. Let cool completely in the machine.

*After measuring out what is needed for this recipe, be sure to replenish your sourdough starter with equal amounts of flour and water.

Quinoa, Millet, and Raisin Bread

Reviving the quinoa grain and introducing it into the United States from Peru was a great by-product of the Peace Corps. Legend has it that a Corps volunteer rediscovered this old Inca staple, loved its taste and texture, and developed an American market for the nutritional grain. This bread is packed with flavor and nutrition and needs only cream cheese, butter, or drained yogurt spread to make a treat for breakfast or a snack.

SMALL LOAF (1 POUND)	INGREDIENTS	LARGE LOAF (1½ POUNDS)
¼ cup	millet meal	⅓ cup
⅓ cup	boiling water	½ cup
1½ teaspoons	active dry yeast	2¼ teaspoons
1¾ cups	bread flour	2⅔ cups
¾ cup	cooked quinoa	1 cup plus 2 tablespoons
½ teaspoon	ground cloves	¾ teaspoon
½ teaspoon	salt	¾ teaspoon
2 tablespoons	brown sugar	3 tablespoons
½ cup	water	¾ cup
½ cup	raisins	¾ cup

1. In a small saucepan, cook the millet in ⅓ (½) cup boiling water 5 minutes. Remove from the heat and let cool.

2. Add all ingredients except the raisins (but including the millet) in the order suggested by your bread machine manual and process on the bread cycle according to the manufacturer's directions.

3. At the beeper (or at the end of the first kneading in the Panasonic, National, and Sanyo), add the raisins.

Quinoa Bread
(Keke de Quinoa)

A platter of sliced mango, pineapple, or berries and this sweet quinoa loaf taste of tropical sunshine and turquoise blue water. Sweet but nutritious, this sultry loaf is a powerful package of vitamins and protein.

SMALL LOAF (1 POUND)	INGREDIENTS	LARGE LOAF (1½ POUNDS)
1½ teaspoons	active dry yeast	2¼ teaspoons
1½ cups	bread flour	2¼ cups
¾ cup	cooked quinoa	1 cup plus 2 tablespoons
½ cup	brown sugar	¾ cup
1 teaspoon	ground cinnamon	1½ teaspoons
½ teaspoon	ground cloves	¾ teaspoon
½ teaspoon	salt	¾ teaspoon
½ cup	chopped walnuts	¾ cup
1 teaspoon	vanilla extract	1½ teaspoons
2 tablespoons	vegetable oil	3 tablespoons
2	whole eggs	3
⅓ cup	water	½ cup

Add all ingredients in the order suggested by your bread machine manual and process on the bread cycle according to the manufacturer's directions.

Chocolate Cinnamon Bread

Chocolate is so subtle. It is as much scent as flavor, not sweet. This is a light bread, good first thing in the morning with fruit and coffee and later in the day with milk or tea. Make a peanut butter sandwich with it or just skim coat it with bitter-orange marmalade for the adults.

SMALL LOAF (1 POUND)	INGREDIENTS	LARGE LOAF (1½ POUNDS)
¾ cup plus 2 tablespoons	hot brewed coffee	1¼ cups
¼ cup	unsweetened cocoa powder	⅓ cup
1½ teaspoons	active dry yeast	2¼ teaspoons
1¾ cups	bread flour	2⅔ cups
⅓ cup	whole wheat flour	½ cup
2 tablespoons	sugar	3 tablespoons
½ teaspoon	salt	¾ teaspoon
1 teaspoon	ground cinnamon	1½ teaspoons
2 tablespoons	vegetable oil	3 tablespoons

1. Pour the hot coffee into a small bowl. Add the cocoa and stir until dissolved and smooth. Let cool to room temperature.

2. Add all ingredients in the order suggested by your bread machine manual and process on the bread cycle according to the manufacturer's directions.

Dalpuri

When the British shipped indentured servants from India to work the sugarcane crops of Trinidad, the Indians brought this filled flat bread with them. Now it is part of island cooking. Crispy dalpuri *with its surprise split pea filling makes a fine hors d'oeuvre.*

Yield: 4 (7-inch) flat breads

FILLING

1 cup	water
½ cup	dried yellow split peas
½ teaspoon	salt
1 teaspoon	ground cumin
⅛ teaspoon	ground black pepper

DOUGH

1½ teaspoons	active dry yeast
2 cups	bread flour
½ teaspoon	salt
1 tablespoon	vegetable oil
¾ cup	water

1. Bring 1 cup of water to a boil. Add the split peas and simmer 30 minutes. Drain the peas and mash by hand or puree in a food processor. Add the salt, cumin, and black pepper. Let the filling cool.

2. Add all ingredients for the dough in the order suggested by your bread machine manual and process on the dough cycle according to the manufacturer's directions.

3. At the end of the dough cycle, remove the dough from the machine and divide into 4 equal parts. Roll each piece of dough into a ball. With your fingers, make a large indentation in each piece. Add 2 tablespoons of filling and pull the dough up around the filling, pinching the ends together securely to seal. Grease the bottom of a skillet or heavy saucepan and use it press down each ball of dough until it is a round less than ½ inch thick.

4. In a nonstick or lightly greased frying pan, cook the *dalpuri* over medium heat 10 minutes on each side, or until golden brown and cooked through. Eat warm, sliced into wedges.

Brazilian Empanadas

Hopefully, this recipe will begin the creative empanada experience. Once you have the timing of this process and the basic dough, change the shape and filling of the empanadas. They make great hors d'oeuvres and snacks, allowing you to use leftovers to their best advantage. To do ahead, freeze fully formed empanadas and bake them off just before your next impromptu cocktail party.

Yield: 16 to 18 hors d'oeuvre-size empanadas

DOUGH

1½ teaspoons	active dry yeast
1¾ cups	bread flour
½ cup	yellow cornmeal
1 tablespoon	sugar
½ teaspoon	salt
1 tablespoon	vegetable oil
1 cup	water

FILLING

½ cup	minced onion
1 tablespoon	olive oil
1	garlic clove, minced
1 cup	chopped cooked chicken or meat
½ teaspoon	salt
½ teaspoon	dried oregano
1 teaspoon	red wine vinegar

⅛ teaspoon	ground black pepper
¼ cup	raisins
¼ cup	chopped green olives

1. Add all ingredients for the dough in the order suggested by your bread machine manual and process on the dough cycle according to the manufacturer's directions.
2. While the dough is being processed, make the filling. In a medium skillet, sauté the onion in the olive oil over medium heat until translucent, about 3 minutes. Stir in the garlic and cook 1 minute; remove from the heat. Add all other ingredients and mix. Let cool to room temperature.
3. At the end of the dough cycle, remove the dough from the machine. Preheat the oven to 375 degrees. On a floured board with a floured rolling pin, roll out the dough ¼ inch thick. With a 2½-inch cookie cutter or a glass, cut out circles. Place 1 tablespoon filling on the left side of each circle. Fold the right side over to form a semicircle. Firmly pinch the edges together to seal. Place the turnovers on a nonstick or lightly greased baking sheet. Set in a draftfree place, cover, and let rise 20 minutes. With a scissors, snip a cross in the center of each empanada. This will help prevent the turnover from popping open along its side. Bake 15 to 20 minutes, until lightly browned. Eat hot or at room temperature.

Venezuelan Banana Bread

I've adapted this bread from a Venezuelan cake, which contains these rich and fruity ingredients. The bread machine helps lighten the texture and emphasizes the intense banana-cinnamon flavor.

SMALL LOAF (1 POUND)	INGREDIENTS	LARGE LOAF (1½ POUNDS)
¼ cup	ricotta	⅓ cup
1½ teaspoons	active dry yeast	2¼ teaspoons
1¾ cups	bread flour	2⅔ cups
½ cup	yellow cornmeal	¾ cup
¼ cup	brown sugar	⅓ cup
1 teaspoon	ground cinnamon	1½ teaspoons
1 teaspoon	salt	1½ teaspoons
⅔ cup	water	1 cup
½ cup	diced banana	¾ cup
2 teaspoons	butter	1 tablespoon

1. Drain the ricotta in a sieve ½ hour.

2. Add all ingredients except the banana and butter in the order suggested by your bread machine manual and process on the bread cycle according to the manufacturer's directions.

3. In a small skillet, sauté the diced banana in the butter over medium-high heat 1 to 2 minutes, stirring gently, until barely browned. Remove to a plate and set aside.

4. At the beeper (or at the end of the first kneading in the Panasonic, National, and Sanyo), add the banana.

Corn Bread with Fruit and Spice

Warm slices of this unusual bread slathered with butter or cottage cheese will help you start the day bright eyed. The hot and sweet flavors of the Yucatán, from oranges and bananas, cumin and cloves, create a vacation bread, a change of pace from the daily routine. It is loaded with vitamins, calcium, and protein.

SMALL LOAF (1 POUND)	INGREDIENTS	LARGE LOAF (1½ POUNDS)
1½ teaspoons	active dry yeast	2¼ teaspoons
2 cups	bread flour	3 cups
½ cup	yellow cornmeal	¾ cup
2 tablespoons	powdered milk	3 tablespoons
½ cup	mashed banana	¾ cup
½ teaspoon	dried oregano	¾ teaspoon
½ teaspoon	ground cumin	¾ teaspoon
¼ teaspoon	ground cloves	¼ teaspoon
¼ teaspoon	ground cinnamon	½ teaspoon
¼ teaspoon	ground black pepper	½ teaspoon
1 tablespoon	grated orange zest	1½ tablespoons
½ teaspoon	salt	¾ teaspoon
2 tablespoons	sugar	3 tablespoons
⅔ cup	water	1 cup

Add all ingredients in the order suggested by your bread machine manual and process on the bread cycle according to the manufacturer's directions.

Bermuda Fruitcake

Giving a Bermuda fruitcake to everyone on your holiday gift list will take less of your time and money and be more personal than just about any other present. Wrap with clear cellophane and two colors of curling ribbon.

SMALL LOAF (1 POUND)	INGREDIENTS	LARGE LOAF (1½ POUNDS)
¼ cup	golden raisins	⅓ cup
¼ cup	currants	⅓ cup
½ cup	chopped pecans or walnuts	¾ cup
½ cup	amber or dark rum	¾ cup
1½ teaspoons	active dry yeast	2¼ teaspoons
2 cups	bread flour	3 cups
2 tablespoons	sugar	3 tablespoons
½ teaspoon	grated nutmeg	¾ teaspoon
½ teaspoon	ground cinnamon	¾ teaspoon
1 teaspoon	ground ginger	1½ teaspoons
½ teaspoon	salt	¾ teaspoon
2 tablespoons	molasses	3 tablespoons
2 tablespoons	butter	3 tablespoons
2	eggs	3
2 tablespoons	candied lemon zest (recipe follows)	3 tablespoons
⅔ cup	water	1 cup

1. Soak the raisins, currants, and nuts in the rum ½ hour. Drain, reserving the rum.
2. Add all ingredients except the rum, raisins, currants, and nuts in the order suggested by your bread machine manual and process on the bread cycle according to the manufacturer's directions.
3. At the beeper (or at the end of the first kneading in the Panasonic, Sanyo, and National), add the raisins, currants, and nuts. Save the rum.
4. When you remove the bread from the machine at the end of the baking cycle, brush the warm loaf with some of the reserved rum. When the bread is completely cool, brush again with the remaining rum.

Candied Lemon or Orange Zest

With a swivel-bladed vegetable peeler, remove the colored zest from 4 lemons or 2 oranges, leaving behind the bitter white pith. In a small saucepan, bring 1 cup sugar and 1 cup water to a boil, swirling the pan to dissolve the sugar. Add the zest, reduce the heat to medium, and simmer 5 minutes. Let the zest cool in the syrup, then transfer to a covered jar and refrigerate for up to 3 weeks. To use, lift the zest from the syrup with a fork or slotted spoon and drain off as much syrup as possible. Mince the candied zest before adding to a bread recipe. Makes ¼ cup.

Orange and Chocolate Bread

This tea bread can also be a sweet dessert when melted chocolate is drizzled over the top. For another variation, brush with orange liqueur, such as Curaçao, and glaze with warm apricot jam.

SMALL LOAF (1 POUND)	INGREDIENTS	LARGE LOAF (1½ POUNDS)
1½ teaspoons	active dry yeast	2¼ teaspoons
2 cups	bread flour	3 cups
2 tablespoons	wheat germ	3 tablespoons
½ cup	unsweetened cocoa powder	¾ cup
2 tablespoons	grated orange zest	3 tablespoons
1 teaspoon	ground cinnamon	1½ teaspoons
⅓ cup	sugar	½ cup
½ teaspoon	salt	¾ teaspoon
2 tablespoons	vegetable oil	3 tablespoons
1	whole egg	1
0	egg yolk	1
¾ cup	water	1 cup plus 2 tablespoons

Add all ingredients in the order suggested by your bread machine manual and process on the bread cycle according to the manufacturer's directions.

Jamaican Pineapple, Molasses, and Ginger Bread

As soon as it is cool enough to handle, slice this caramel-crusted loaf thick to serve with ice cream or with a refreshing tall drink.

SMALL LOAF (1 POUND)	INGREDIENTS	LARGE LOAF (1½ POUNDS)
1¼ teaspoons	active dry yeast	1¾ teaspoons
1¾ cups	bread flour	2⅔ cups
½ cup	whole wheat flour	¾ cup
½ teaspoon	salt	¾ teaspoon
2 teaspoons	minced fresh ginger	1 tablespoon
2 tablespoons	vegetable oil	3 tablespoons
3 tablespoons	molasses	¼ cup
½ cup	water	¾ cup
½ cup	unsweetened pineapple chunks	⅔ cup
2 tablespoons	rum (optional)	3 tablespoons

1. Add all ingredients except the pineapple and rum in the order suggested by your bread machine manual and process on the bread cycle according to the manufacturer's directions.

2. If using canned pineapple, drain completely. Do not use crushed pineapple. Fresh pineapple should be cut into ½-inch dice.

3. At the beeper (or at the end of the first kneading in the Panasonic, Sanyo, and National), add the pineapple.

4. If you want a taste of rum, brush it on the bread after it has been baked and removed from the machine.

Curried Sweet Potato and Peanut Bread

In Martinique and Guadeloupe baking powder instead of yeast gives this bread its rise. It is served with spicy stew or fish. A tad sweet and barely spicy, it is surprisingly nutritious. Try a slice with cold milk or hot tea or alongside plain yogurt.

SMALL LOAF (1 POUND)	INGREDIENTS	LARGE LOAF (1½ POUNDS)
1½ teaspoons	active dry yeast	2¼ teaspoons
1¾ cups	bread flour	2⅔ cups
½ cup	whole wheat flour	¾ cup
2 tablespoons	wheat bran	3 tablespoons
½ teaspoon	curry powder	¾ teaspoon
¼ cup	flaked coconut	⅓ cup
1 teaspoon	salt	1½ teaspoons
3 tablespoons	molasses	¼ cup
1 tablespoon	vegetable oil	1½ tablespoons
⅓ cup	mashed cooked sweet potato	½ cup
⅔ cup	water	1 cup
¼ cup	unsalted peanuts, chopped	⅓ cup

1. Add all ingredients except the peanuts in the order suggested by your bread machine manual and process on the bread cycle according to the manufacturer's directions.

2. At the beeper (or at the end of the first kneading in the Panasonic, Sanyo, and National), add the peanuts.

Sweet Potato and Coconut Bread

Any time of day, this moist bread will satisfy cravings for something hearty, something sweet. Even though the recipe comes from a sunny island climate, slices are as pleasing spread with cream cheese on a winter morning as they are plain eaten under a beach umbrella.

SMALL LOAF (1 POUND)	INGREDIENTS	LARGE LOAF (1½ POUNDS)
1½ teaspoons	active dry yeast	2¼ teaspoons
1¾ cups	bread flour	2⅔ cups
¼ cup	yellow cornmeal	⅓ cup
½ cup	mashed cooked sweet potato	¾ cup
3 tablespoons	molasses	¼ cup
½ teaspoon	salt	¾ teaspoon
1 tablespoon	vegetable oil	1½ tablespoons
½ cup	unsweetened coconut milk	¾ cup
¼ cup	water	⅓ cup
¼ cup	flaked coconut	⅓ cup

1. Add all ingredients except the flaked coconut in the order suggested by your bread machine manual and process on the bread cycle according to the manufacturer's directions.
2. At the beeper (or at the end of the first kneading in the Panasonic, Sanyo, and National), add the flaked coconut.

Mole Bread

Mole (mo lay) is a complex sauce made of fruits, spices, and unsweetened chocolate. Added to dough, it results in a full-flavored bread.

SMALL LOAF (1 POUND)	INGREDIENTS	LARGE LOAF (1½ POUNDS)
½ teaspoon	hot pepper flakes	¾ teaspoon
¼ cup	sliced almonds	⅓ cup
⅓ cup	chopped onion	½ cup
2 teaspoons	tomato paste	1 tablespoon
2 tablespoons	raisins	3 tablespoons
1 tablespoon	sesame seeds	1½ tablespoons
1	garlic clove(s), minced	1½
¼ teaspoon	ground cinnamon	½ teaspoon
¼ teaspoon	ground cloves	¼ teaspoon
¼ teaspoon	ground coriander	½ teaspoon
¼ teaspoon	aniseed	½ teaspoon
2 tablespoons	unsweetened cocoa powder	3 tablespoons
1½ teaspoons	active dry yeast	2¼ teaspoons
1¾ cups	bread flour	2⅔ cups
½ cup	whole wheat flour	¾ cup
1 teaspoon	salt	1½ teaspoons
⅔ cup	water	1 cup

1. Add all ingredients from hot pepper flakes to cocoa to a food processor. Process until a paste forms. This is the mole.

2. Add all ingredients in the order suggested by your bread machine manual, adding the mole with the water, and process on the bread cycle according to the manufacturer's directions.

Trinidad Hot Cross Buns

Yield: 12 buns

DOUGH

1½ teaspoons	active dry yeast
2 cups	bread flour
¼ cup	brown sugar
2 tablespoons	powdered milk
½ teaspoon	ground cinnamon
¼ teaspoon	grated nutmeg
1 teaspoon	salt
¼ cup	vegetable oil
¾ cup plus 2 tablespoons	water

FILLING AND GLAZE

¾ cup	currants
1 tablespoon	melted butter
1 tablespoon	sugar

1. Add all ingredients for the dough in the order suggested by your bread machine manual and process on the dough cycle according to the manufacturer's directions.
2. At the end of the dough cycle, remove the dough from the machine. Preheat the oven to 350 degrees. Divide the dough into 12 buns. On a floured board, knead 1 tablespoon currants into each bun. Place 1 inch apart on a lightly greased baking sheet. Brush with melted butter and sprinkle with sugar. Let rise 20 minutes.
3. With a sharp knife or single-edged razor blade, gently slice a cross in the top of each bun. Bake 15 to 20 minutes, until brown.

Trinidad Sweet Bread

When Trinidadian Joyce Phillip gave me her recipe, she said, "Use any citrus fruit but lemon. We use orange or lime in our breads and cakes, because we do not have tasty lemons." If you would rather not use coconut milk, she suggests substituting cow's milk in the fruity bread she bakes for breakfast.

SMALL LOAF (1 POUND)	INGREDIENTS	LARGE LOAF (1½ POUNDS)
1½ teaspoons	active dry yeast	2¼ teaspoons
2 cups	bread flour	3 cups
¼ cup	sugar	⅓ cup
1 teaspoon	salt	1½ teaspoons
2 teaspoons	grated orange zest	1 tablespoon
4 tablespoons	unsalted butter	6 tablespoons
1	whole egg	1
0	egg white	1
½ cup	unsweetened coconut milk	¾ cup
¼ cup	pineapple chunks, drained	⅓ cup
2 tablespoons	water	3 tablespoons
¼ cup	raisins	⅓ cup

1. Add all ingredients except the raisins in the order suggested by your bread machine manual and process on the bread cycle according to the manufacturer's directions.

2. At the beeper (or at the end of the first kneading in the Panasonic, Sanyo, and National), add the raisins.

Chapter Seven
Breads of the Middle East

In the Arab world, pita and other flat breads reign supreme. They are quickly baked, easily stored, and light to carry—good breads in the desert. Fresh pita, all puffed up awaiting a filling of highly seasoned vegetables and perhaps some lamb, or for dipping in yogurt or hummus, is one of the great breads of the world. Pitas have become so popular in the United States that giant food conglomerates bake and distribute them. But do not buy pitas in a plastic sack. You and your bread machine will make them so much better, lightly charred and crisp.

Since there are relatively few breads in this part of the world, I have taken culinary license in this chapter to use the produce and typical ingredients of the Middle East—dates, almonds, yogurt—to make higher yeast breads that are not traditional. Nonetheless, I am sure you will enjoy these loaves that incorporate the fragrance and flavors of countries that range from Turkey to Egypt.

Armenian Pita Bread

This high-rise, crisp, chewy pita can be cut in half and filled with tuna, tossed salad, chopped vegetables, or a shish kebab. Or tear it into pieces just large enough to dip in hummus or salsa. It is so much better than store bought.

Yield: 8 pitas

DOUGH

2½ teaspoons	active dry yeast
2 cups	bread flour
1½ teaspoons	salt
1½ teaspoons	sugar
1 cup	water

1. Add all ingredients for the dough in the order suggested by your bread machine manual and process on the dough cycle according to the manufacturer's directions.
2. Preheat the oven to 450 degrees. At the end of the dough cycle, remove the dough from the machine. The dough will be sticky. Divide the dough into 8 pieces. Roll each piece between your hands into a ball.
3. On a floured board with floured hands, press each ball into a 5-inch circle. Place on lightly greased baking sheets. *Do not let rise.* Immediately bake 12 to 15 minutes, until each pita puffs and browns.

Whole Wheat Pita

As is for sandwiches or dipping, or toasted for munching, this pita bread is full of nutty flavor, vitamins, and fiber. Fill with peanut butter or with sliced egg, tomato, and other raw vegetables.

Yield: 8 pitas

DOUGH

2½ teaspoons	active dry yeast
1 cup	whole wheat flour
1¼ cups	bread flour
1 teaspoon	salt
1 teaspoon	sugar
1 cup	water

1. Add all ingredients for the dough in the order suggested by your bread machine manual and process on the dough cycle according to the manufacturer's directions.
2. Preheat the oven to 450 degrees. At the end of the dough cycle, remove the dough from the machine. The dough will be sticky. Roll each piece between your hands to form a ball.
3. On a floured board with floured hands, press each ball into a 5-inch circle. Place on lightly greased baking sheets. *Do not let rise.* Immediately bake until each pita puffs and browns, about 15 minutes.

Egyptian Semit

Semit look like giant seeded bagels, but the crust is crunchier and the inside softer. You need not boil *semit* before baking as you do bagels. For a party, slice the bread horizontally, fill with salmon mousse or chicken liver pâté, cover with the seed-encrusted top, and slice the ring vertically into tiny sandwiches. Or place a small whole cheese, such as a Brie, in the center of the bread ring and small bunches of grapes around the outside for the simplest of desserts.

Yield: 2 (9-inch) or 5 (7-inch) semit

1½ teaspoons	active dry yeast
2 cups	bread flour
2 teaspoons	powdered milk
1 teaspoon	salt
1 tablespoon	vegetable oil or clarified butter
¾ cup plus 2 tablespoons	water
½ cup	sesame seeds

1. Add all ingredients except the sesame seeds in the order suggested by your bread machine manual and process on the dough cycle according to the manufacturer's directions. Preheat the oven to 400 degrees.

2. At the end of the dough cycle, remove the dough from the bread machine. Divide in half for large semit or in 5 pieces for smaller rings. Roll each of the larger pieces into a 24-inch length and form into a ring, pinching the ends to seal the circle. For individual semit, roll each of the 5 pieces into a 15-inch rope and form into 7-inch rings.

3. Pour the sesame seeds into a large, shallow pan. Brush each ring of dough with water and press into the seeds. Turn, dampen the other side, and press that side into the sesame seeds. Set the rings on lightly greased baking sheets and let rise in a draftfree place 20 minutes, or until doubled in size.

4. Place the semit in the oven. Immediately reduce the heat to 350 degrees and bake 20 minutes, or until golden brown.

Turkish Yogurt Bread

With fresh or cooked fruit, eggs, or peanut butter, this sweet, tangy bread tastes especially good early in the day drizzled with honey and sprinkled with wheat germ or chopped nuts. It is packed with vitamins, fiber, protein, and calcium.

SMALL LOAF (1 POUND)	INGREDIENTS	LARGE LOAF (1½ POUNDS)
1¼ teaspoons	active dry yeast	1¾ teaspoons
1⅔ cups	bread flour	2½ cups
½ cup	whole wheat flour	¾ cup
½ teaspoon	salt	¾ teaspoon
¼ cup	honey	⅓ cup
¼ cup	plain yogurt	⅓ cup
1 tablespoon	vegetable oil	1½ tablespoons
½ cup	water	¾ cup

Add all ingredients in the order suggested by your bread machine manual and process on the bread cycle according to the manufacturer's directions.

Bulgur Bread with Lebanese Zatar

Zatar is a Middle Eastern spice mix used with meats and flat breads.

SMALL LOAF (1 POUND)	INGREDIENTS	LARGE LOAF (1½ POUNDS)
½ cup	bulgur wheat	¾ cup
1 cup	boiling water	1½ cups
1½ teaspoons	active dry yeast	2¼ teaspoons
1¾ cups	bread flour	2⅔ cups
1 teaspoon	salt	1½ teaspoons
¾ cup plus 1 tablespoon	water	1 cup plus 2 tablespoons

ZATAR		
1 teaspoon	dried thyme	1½ teaspoons
2 teaspoons	sesame seeds	1 tablespoon
½ teaspoon	dried marjoram	¾ teaspoon
½ teaspoon	ground allspice	¾ teaspoon
1 tablespoon	ground almonds	1½ tablespoons
1 tablespoon	grated lemon zest	1½ tablespoons
2 tablespoons	olive oil	3 tablespoons

1. Place the bulgur in a small heatproof bowl. Pour on 1 (1½) cup(s) boiling water and let stand until the mixture cools to room temperature.
2. In a small bowl, mix all the zatar ingredients together to form a paste.
3. Add all ingredients including the zatar paste in the order suggested by your bread machine manual and process on the bread cycle according to the manufacturer's directions.

Iranian Spinach and Yogurt Bread
(Borani)

This bread with greens, fiber, and calcium is very good for you and tastes mild enough to eat with meats, curried chicken, or egg salad. A 10-ounce package of frozen spinach will yield about ¾ cup.

SMALL LOAF (1 POUND)	INGREDIENTS	LARGE LOAF (1½ POUNDS)
½ cup	thawed frozen chopped spinach, squeezed dry	¾ cup
1½ teaspoons	active dry yeast	2¼ teaspoons
1¾ cups	bread flour	2⅔ cups
½ cup	whole wheat flour	¾ cup
2 tablespoons	wheat germ	3 tablespoons
1 tablespoon	sugar	1½ tablespoons
1 teaspoon	salt	1½ teaspoons
¼ cup	minced onion	⅓ cup
¼ cup	plain yogurt	⅓ cup
1	whole egg	1
0	egg yolk	1
⅓ cup	water	½ cup
½ teaspoon	sesame seeds	¾ teaspoon

1. In a piece of cheesecloth or a kitchen towel, squeeze as much moisture as you can out of the spinach.
2. Add all ingredients except the sesame seeds in the order suggested by your bread machine manual and process on the bread cycle according to the manufacturer's directions.
3. During the final rising, sprinkle the sesame seeds on top.

Syrian Date and Almond Bread

The spicy, sweet date mixture brings to mind Bedouin tents rather than Syrian city life. It tastes right with mint tea, iced or hot. No need for butter; the bread is very moist. No need for jam; the bread is sweet and fruity. For sandwiches, fill with a little cream cheese or drained yogurt.

SMALL LOAF (1 POUND)	INGREDIENTS	LARGE LOAF (1½ POUNDS)
1½ teaspoons	active dry yeast	2¼ teaspoons
2 cups	bread flour	3 cups
3 tablespoons	wheat bran	¼ cup
2 tablespoons	sugar	3 tablespoons
½ teaspoon	ground cinnamon	¾ teaspoon
¼ teaspoon	ground cloves	½ teaspoon
½ teaspoon	salt	¾ teaspoon
¼ teaspoon	ground black pepper	½ teaspoon
¾ cup plus 2 tablespoons	water	1¼ cups
½ cup	chopped dates	¾ cup
¼ cup	sliced almonds	⅓ cup

1. Add all ingredients except the dates and almonds in the order suggested by your bread machine manual and process on the bread cycle according to the manufacturer's directions.
2. At the beeper (or at the end of the first kneading in the Panasonic, Sanyo, and National), add the dates and almonds.

Syrian Hard Rolls
(Kaak)

A kaak is a cross between a bagel and a doughnut. Sweet and spicy, they are excellent with coffee, even dunked in it. A basketful would make a fine gift.

Yield: 12 to 15 rolls

DOUGH

1¼ teaspoons	active dry yeast
2 cups	bread flour
¼ teaspoon	sugar
1½ teaspoons	salt
¾ teaspoon	aniseed
½ teaspoon	ground cumin
½ teaspoon	ground coriander
¼ cup	vegetable oil
1	egg, beaten
⅔ cup	water
2 tablespoons	sesame seeds

GLAZE

1	egg, beaten

1. Add all ingredients for the dough except the sesame seeds in the order suggested by your bread machine manual and process on the dough cycle according to the manufacturer's directions.

2. At the end of the dough cycle, remove the dough from the machine. Cut into pieces the size of Ping-Pong balls. You will have more than a dozen pieces. Roll each piece into a 6-inch rope and twist around your hand into a circle, pinching the ends together to seal.

3. Place the rings on a lightly greased baking sheet. Brush with the second beaten egg. Sprinkle with the sesame seeds. Let rise 1 hour in a draftfree place.

4. Meanwhile, preheat the oven to 375 degrees. Bake 15 minutes. Reduce the oven temperature to 325 and bake 10 minutes longer, until lightly browned.

Syrian Meat Pie

While you could call this a pizza, it is actually a Syrian bread called khobiz. *Topped with meat and served with the yogurt ubiquitous in the Middle East, its delicate spicing and lack of cheese make it decidedly different. Serve as a main course or an hors d'oeuvre.*

Yield: 2 medium pies

DOUGH

1½ teaspoons	active dry yeast
2 cups	bread flour
1 teaspoon	sugar
½ teaspoon	salt
1 tablespoon	vegetable oil
¾ cup plus 2 tablespoons	water

TOPPING

1	onion, chopped
1 tablespoon	olive oil
1	garlic clove, minced
½ pound	ground beef
½ teaspoon	ground allspice
2 tablespoons	tomato paste
2 tablespoons	dry red wine or water
¼ teaspoon	salt
⅛ teaspoon	ground black pepper
1 cup	plain yogurt

1. Add all ingredients for the dough in the order suggested by your bread machine manual and process on the dough cycle according to the manufacturer's directions.
2. In a medium skillet, cook the onion in the olive oil over medium heat until translucent, about 3 minutes. Add the garlic and beef. Cook, stirring to break up lumps, until the beef browns, about 3 minutes longer. Add the allspice, tomato paste, wine or water, salt, and pepper. Cover and cook over low heat 15 minutes.
3. At the end of the dough cycle, remove the dough from the machine. Preheat the oven to 450 degrees.
4. Divide the dough in half. On a floured board with a floured rolling pin, roll each piece of dough into a 10- to 12-inch circle. Place on a nonstick or lightly greased baking sheet. Let rest 10 minutes, lightly covered.
5. Bake 15 to 20 minutes, until the bread is brown where puffed. As soon as you remove the crusts from the oven, cover each with meat sauce. Serve hot or at room temperature, with yogurt on the side.

Prune and Ginger Bread

The sweet and pungent flavor of this bread lets it stand on its own for breakfast or for a snack later in the day. Slices make an intensively flavored curried chicken open-face or tea sandwich.

SMALL LOAF (1 POUND)	INGREDIENTS	LARGE LOAF (1½ POUNDS)
1½ teaspoons	active dry yeast	2¼ teaspoons
1⅔ cups	bread flour	2½ cups
½ cup	whole wheat flour	¾ cup
2 tablespoons	sugar	3 tablespoons
½ teaspoon	salt	¾ teaspoon
1 teaspoon	minced fresh ginger	1½ teaspoons
½ cup	chopped pitted prunes	¾ cup
1 tablespoon	vegetable oil	1½ tablespoons
¾ cup	water	1 cup plus 2 tablespoons

Add all ingredients in the order suggested by your bread machine manual and process on the basic bread cycle according to the manufacturer's directions.

Turkish Walnut and Honey Bread

Here's a loaf that is sweet, but not too sweet, for breakfast; moist, yet with no fat except for the oil in the walnuts. Since it does not need butter or filling and has enough fruit flavor to stand on its own, this is an excellent picnic bread to eat under blue skies with cool drinks or a slice of melon.

SMALL LOAF (1 POUND)	INGREDIENTS	LARGE LOAF (1½ POUNDS)
1½ teaspoons	active dry yeast	2¼ teaspoons
1¾ cups	bread flour	2⅔ cups
½ cup	whole wheat flour	¾ cup
1 teaspoon	salt	1½ teaspoons
1 tablespoon	grated orange zest	1½ tablespoons
¼ cup	honey	⅓ cup
½ cup	chopped walnuts	¾ cup
¾ cup	water	1 cup plus 2 tablespoons

Add all ingredients in the order suggested by your bread machine manual and process on the bread cycle according to the manufacturer's directions.

Chapter Eight
Breads of India and Asia

Since raised yeast breads are not common to most Asian cuisines, in this chapter I have used bread to capture the flavors of India and the nations of the Pacific, including China, Thailand, and Vietnam. Tandoori seasonings, Indonesian lemongrass and coconut, and Thai fried garlic cover and fill these untraditional yeast breads. Only the flavors are characteristic of their native Asian cuisines. The Indian *naan* is authentic and similar to, but more flavorful than, pita.

In this chapter you will also find a *dim sum* party from the bread machine, a Chinese hors d'oeuvre buffet of shrimp toast and two kinds of dumplings. One batch of dough can be divided in half for two types of dumplings. After you remove the dough from the bread machine, start the shrimp toast and process on the bread cycle. Fill the dumplings. When guests arrive, steam and bake the dumplings and toast the shrimp bread. With an hour's work in advance and another half hour for steaming, baking, and toasting, you will be amazed to have created your own dim sum.

Philippine Banana, Brown Sugar, and Anise Bread

This high, light, yet elastic loaf is mildly sweet, mildly spicy, mildly nutty. Make a sophisticated peanut butter or sliced chicken sandwich with it or sprinkle with sugar and coconut and broil just long enough to caramelize the sugar and toast the coconut.

SMALL LOAF (1 POUND)	INGREDIENTS	LARGE LOAF (1½ POUNDS)
1½ teaspoons	active dry yeast	2¼ teaspoons
1¾ cups	bread flour	2⅔ cups
½ cup	whole wheat flour	¾ cup
3 tablespoons	brown sugar	¼ cup
1 teaspoon	salt	1½ teaspoons
1 teaspoon	aniseed	1½ teaspoons
1 tablespoon	vegetable oil	1½ tablespoons
½ cup	mashed banana	¾ cup
⅔ cup	water	1 cup

Add all ingredients in the order suggested by your bread machine manual and process on the bread cycle according to the manufacturer's directions.

Chickpea and Potato Bread

It is soft and subtly spiced, best plain while still warm. Toast it and top with grilled eggplant and pepper or sliced tomato and cold lamb or chicken. To serve with curry, slice very thin, cut into triangles, and toast in the oven.

SMALL LOAF (1 POUND)	INGREDIENTS	LARGE LOAF (1½ POUNDS)
1½ teaspoons	active dry yeast	2¼ teaspoons
1½ cups	bread flour	2¼ cups
½ cup	whole wheat flour	¾ cup
½ teaspoon	ground cumin	¾ teaspoon
½ teaspoon	ground coriander	¾ teaspoon
⅛ teaspoon	cayenne pepper	¼ teaspoon
1 teaspoon	salt	1½ teaspoons
2 teaspoons	sugar	1 tablespoon
½ cup	mashed potato	¾ cup
½ cup	chopped raw onion	¾ cup
½ cup	water	¾ cup
½ cup	canned chickpeas	¾ cup

1. Add all ingredients except the chickpeas in the order suggested by your bread machine manual and process on the bread cycle according to the manufacturer's directions.

2. Drain and rinse the chickpeas; drain again.

3. At the beeper (or at the end of the first kneading in the Panasonic, Sanyo, and National), add the chickpeas.

Coconut and Date Bread

The sweetness of the dates, the zip of the ginger, the aroma of the fennel, and the texture of the coconut make up a complex bread interesting enough to be eaten plain or for dessert with a fruit salad or wedge of melon.

SMALL LOAF (1 POUND)	INGREDIENTS	LARGE LOAF (1½ POUNDS)
1½ teaspoons	active dry yeast	2¼ teaspoons
1¾ cups	bread flour	2⅔ cups
½ cup	whole wheat flour	¾ cup
2 tablespoons	sugar	3 tablespoons
1 teaspoon	salt	1½ teaspoons
1 teaspoon	minced fresh ginger	1½ teaspoons
1 teaspoon	fennel seeds	1½ teaspoons
½ cup	chopped dates	¾ cup
½ cup	plain yogurt	¾ cup
½ cup	water	¾ cup
½ cup	flaked coconut	¾ cup

1. Add all ingredients except the coconut in the order suggested by your bread machine manual and process on the bread cycle according to the manufacturer's directions.

2. At the beeper (or at the end of the first kneading in the Panasonic, Sanyo, and National), add the coconut.

Indonesian Coconut and Lemongrass Bread

This bread is best at or after sunset, definitely not for breakfast. Its assertive garlic flavor complements soups with noodles and vegetables. Serve toasted with slices cut into fingers as an hors d'oeuvre, or make croutons out of leftovers to toss into salads.

SMALL LOAF (1 POUND)	INGREDIENTS	LARGE LOAF (1½ POUNDS)
2	garlic cloves	3
1 tablespoon	vegetable oil	1½ tablespoons
1½ teaspoons	active dry yeast	2¼ teaspoons
1¾ cups	bread flour	2⅔ cups
½ cup	whole wheat flour	¾ cup
1 tablespoon	sugar	1½ tablespoons
1 teaspoon	salt	1½ teaspoons
1 teaspoon	minced fresh ginger	1½ teaspoons
1 teaspoon	thinly sliced lemongrass	1½ teaspoons
⅛ teaspoon	cayenne	⅛ teaspoon
¾ cup plus 2 tablespoons	water	1¼ cups
½ cup	flaked coconut	¾ cup

1. Mince the garlic. Sauté in oil until just golden. Let cool.

2. Add all ingredients except the coconut in the order suggested by your bread machine manual and process on the bread cycle according to the manufacturer's directions.

3. At the beeper (or at the end of the first kneading in the Panasonic, Sanyo, and National), add the flaked coconut.

Thai Fried Garlic and Coconut Bread

This is not a bread made in Thailand; it is a bread with the tastes of Thailand. Slivers of garlic and bits of ginger enliven the bread; coconut gives it a mellow sweetness and added texture. On its own, warm from the machine, this bread is a garlic-lover's hors d'oeuvre, or with Thai or Chinese soups a warming meal.

SMALL LOAF (1 POUND)	INGREDIENTS	LARGE LOAF (1½ POUNDS)
2	garlic cloves	3
2 teaspoons	vegetable oil	1 tablespoon
1½ teaspoons	active dry yeast	2¼ teaspoons
2 cups	bread flour	3 cups
2 tablespoons	wheat bran	3 tablespoons
1 teaspoon	minced fresh ginger	1½ teaspoons
¾ teaspoon	salt	1 teaspoon
1 tablespoon	sugar	1½ tablespoons
2 tablespoons	flaked coconut	3 tablespoons
½ cup	unsweetened coconut milk	¾ cup
⅓ cup	water	½ cup

1. Cut the garlic lengthwise into large, thin slices. In a small skillet, cook the garlic in oil over medium-low heat until just golden, 2 to 3 minutes. Do not let brown, or the garlic will be bitter. Immediately remove to a small bowl and let cool. **2.** Add all ingredients in the order suggested by your bread machine manual and process on the bread cycle according to the manufacturer's directions.

Naan

Although naan *is a classic flat bread of India—the traditional accompaniment to tandoori chicken—you need not eat it with meals alone. Just out of the oven, the* naan *are so delicate and flavorful that they are often nibbled before dinner. Serve with yogurt dips or with any food that has a sauce or gravy, especially curry.*

Yield: 8 naan

DOUGH

2 teaspoons	active dry yeast
2 cups	bread flour
1 teaspoon	sugar
¼ teaspoon	salt
⅛ teaspoon	baking soda
1 tablespoon	vegetable oil
½ cup	plain yogurt
½ cup	milk

TOPPING

2 tablespoons	unsalted butter
2 tablespoons	black sesame seeds*

1. Add all ingredients except the butter and black sesame seeds in the order suggested by your bread machine manual and process on the dough cycle according to the manufacturer's directions.

2. Preheat the oven to 450 degrees. When the dough cycle ends, remove the dough from the machine and divide into 8 pieces. On a floured surface with a floured rolling pin, roll each piece into an 8-by-4-inch oval. Cover and let rise 20 minutes, or until doubled.

3. Melt the butter for the topping. Brush the top of each naan with butter and sprinkle with the sesame seeds. Bake 7 to 10 minutes, or until golden. Lightly brush the bottom of each naan with water, stack, and cover, or eat as soon as they are cool enough to handle.

*If the black sesame seeds sold in Indian and Chinese shops are not available, use regular sesame seeds.

Indonesian Peanut and Coconut Bread

This bread fuses the tastes that come together in Indonesian cuisine: garlic, ginger, coconut, and peanuts. Coconut mellows the other spices without diluting them. The soft bread, dotted with crunchy peanuts, well toasted in thick slices, makes a sensational curried chicken salad sandwich.

SMALL LOAF (1 POUND)	INGREDIENTS	LARGE LOAF (1½ POUNDS)
1 teaspoon	active dry yeast	1½ teaspoons
1½ cups	bread flour	2¼ cups
¾ cup	whole wheat flour	1 cup plus 2 tablespoons
1 teaspoon	minced fresh ginger	1½ teaspoons
1	garlic clove(s), minced	1½
1 tablespoon	sugar	1½ tablespoons
1 teaspoon	salt	1½ teaspoons
1	whole egg	1
0	egg yolk	1
½ cup	unsweetened coconut milk	¾ cup
½ cup	water	¾ cup
⅓ cup	unsalted roasted peanuts, chopped	½ cup

1. Add all ingredients except the peanuts in the order suggested by your bread machine manual and process on the bread cycle according to the manufacturer's directions.

2. At the beeper (or at the end of the first kneading in the Panasonic, Sanyo, and National), add the chopped peanuts.

Yogurt, Banana, and Coconut Bread

The riper the banana, the sweeter the bread. When sliced very thin, this bread is a perfect partner for curries or other Indian food. Sliced thick, its fruitiness is perfect for breakfast or snacks, and it can add new definition to peanut butter sandwiches.

SMALL LOAF (1 POUND)	INGREDIENTS	LARGE LOAF (1½ POUNDS)
1 tablespoon	clarified butter	1½ tablespoons
1½ teaspoons	active dry yeast	2¼ teaspoons
1¾ cups	bread flour	2⅔ cups
½ cup	whole wheat flour	¾ cup
1 tablespoon	sugar	1½ tablespoons
1 teaspoon	salt	1½ teaspoons
1 tablespoon	black mustard seeds or black sesame seeds*	1½ tablespoons
½ cup	mashed banana	¾ cup
½ cup	plain yogurt	¾ cup
½ cup	flaked coconut	¾ cup
¼ cup	water	⅓ cup

Add all ingredients in the order suggested by your bread machine manual and process on the bread cycle according to the manufacturer's directions.

*Both seeds are available from Indian food shops.

Tandoori Bread

In a tandoori oven, yogurt-marinated meat and poultry are baked at very high temperatures to sear the outside while keeping the inside juicy. This recipe uses the tandoori marinade as a spicy coating and a very hot oven for a crusty yet moist bread. With iced tea, beer, or white wine, it makes a lively hors d'oeuvre or snack.

Yield: 2 tandoori rings

DOUGH

1½ teaspoons	active dry yeast
2 cups	bread flour
¼ cup	whole wheat flour
2 tablespoons	vegetable oil
1 teaspoon	salt
1 cup	water

TANDOORI RUB

¼ cup	plain yogurt
1 tablespoon	lemon juice
1 tablespoon	vegetable oil
1 teaspoon	ground ginger
1	garlic clove, minced
1½ teaspoons	*garam masala**
¼ teaspoon	turmeric
⅛ teaspoon	cayenne
1 drop	yellow food coloring
1 drop	red food coloring

1. Add all ingredients for the dough in the order suggested by your bread machine manual and process on the dough cycle according to the manufacturer's directions.

2. Preheat the oven to 450 degrees. In the food processor, puree all the ingredients for the tandoori rub into a paste.

3. At the end of the dough cycle, remove the dough from the machine. Divide in half. Roll each piece into an 18-inch strip. Make each strip into a 7-inch ring. Place on a nonstick or lightly greased baking sheet or on 2 baking sheets that will give them room to rise and bake.

4. Thickly spread the tandoori rub all over the rings. Let the rings rise uncovered in a draftfree place 20 minutes. Gently brush on more tandoori rub. With a sharp knife or single-edged razor blade, cut crosses in the top of the bread rings. Be gentle so the bread does not deflate. Bake 10 to 15 minutes, until the rings look slightly charred.

*Garam masala is an Indian spice mixture. If not available, make your own from equal parts of ground cumin, coriander, cardamom, cinnamon, black pepper, and cloves.

Whole Wheat Bread with Ginger and Cashews

This bread is slightly nutty, slightly spicy, and very healthy, full of calcium, fiber, and vitamins. Toasting maximizes the nutty taste and makes the kitchen smell of ginger. For sandwiches, try sliced eggs or turkey or cucumber, tomato, and sprouts.

SMALL LOAF (1 POUND)	INGREDIENTS	LARGE LOAF (1½ POUNDS)
1½ teaspoons	active dry yeast	2¼ teaspoons
2½ cups	whole wheat flour	3¾ cups
1 teaspoon	minced fresh ginger	1½ teaspoons
1 teaspoon	salt	1½ teaspoons
2 tablespoons	molasses	3 tablespoons
1 tablespoon	vegetable oil	1½ tablespoons
½ cup	plain yogurt	¾ cup
⅔ cup	water	1 cup
½ cup	chopped cashews or unsalted peanuts	¾ cup

1. Add all ingredients except the cashews or peanuts in the order suggested by your bread machine manual and process on the bread cycle according to the manufacturer's directions.

2. At the beeper (or at the end of the first kneading in the Panasonic, Sanyo, and National), add the nuts.

Shrimp Toast

This variation on Chinese shrimp toast can be made ahead in the bread machine, refrigerated for a day or frozen, and toasted just before serving. Note: The ingredients for this recipe should be chilled, not at room temperature.

SMALL LOAF (1 POUND)	INGREDIENTS	LARGE LOAF (1½ POUNDS)
¼ pound	fresh shrimp	⅓ pound
1 tablespoon	vegetable oil	1½ tablespoons
2 teaspoons	minced fresh ginger	1 tablespoon
2	scallions, chopped	3
1½ teaspoons	active dry yeast	2¼ teaspoons
2 cups	bread flour	3 cups
2 teaspoons	sugar	1 tablespoon
½ teaspoon	salt	¾ teaspoon
¾ cup	water	1 cup plus 2 tablespoons
1 teaspoon	Asian sesame oil	1½ teaspoons

1. Shell and coarsely chop the shrimp. In a wok or large frying pan, heat the oil. Add the shrimp and cook over medium-high heat, stirring, until the shrimp turn pink, about 2 minutes. Stir in the ginger and scallions. Transfer to a small bowl, cover, and refrigerate until thoroughly chilled.

2. Add all ingredients except the sesame oil, but including the shrimp, in the order suggested by your bread machine manual and process on the bread cycle according to the manufacturer's directions. Let cool. If not using immediately, refrigerate.

3. Slice cool bread ½ inch thick. Brush lightly with sesame oil. Toast each side in a toaster oven or under a broiler until golden. Cut into triangles and serve hot.

Steamed Meat Dumplings

This dim sum offering miniaturizes the common Chinese steamed bun, equalizing the filling with the dough, to make a tasty hors d'oeuvre. The more traditional version, a large doughy bun with a tiny bit of meat in the center, is too filling to eat American-style. Serve these morsels hot with light soy sauce or rice vinegar for dipping.

Yield: 24 dumplings

DOUGH

2 teaspoons	active dry yeast
2 cups	bread flour
1 teaspoon	sugar
1 teaspoon	salt
1 tablespoon	vegetable oil
¾ cup	water

FILLING

1½ teaspoons	vegetable oil
½ pound	ground beef, pork, turkey, or chicken
¼ teaspoon	salt
1	garlic clove, minced
1 teaspoon	minced fresh ginger
1½ teaspoons	cornstarch
1 tablespoon	soy sauce

---

1. Add all ingredients for the dough in the order suggested by your bread machine manual and process on the dough cycle according to the manufacturer's directions. **2.** In a medium skillet, heat the oil for the filling. Add the meat and cook over medium heat, stirring to break up lumps, until it browns, 3 to 5 minutes. Add the salt, garlic, and ginger. Stir the cornstarch into the soy sauce until it dissolves. Add to the meat mixture and cook until the sauce thickens and is absorbed by the meat, about 1 minute. Remove from the heat and let cool. If the meat renders too much fat, drain the mixture.

3. When the dough cycle ends, remove the dough from the machine and roll into a 2-foot rope. Cut into 24 equal pieces. Roll or stretch each piece into a 3-inch circle. Put 1 teaspoon of meat filling in the center of each circle. Pull the edges up and pinch firmly together to enclose the filling. Repeat with the remaining circles. Turn the dumplings upside down on a greased plate, spaced about 1 inch apart, and let rise 30 minutes.

4. Use a bamboo steamer. If you do not have a steamer, improvise one by setting a greased heatproof dish or pie plate on a ring or a low, empty 7-ounce can in a large frying pan or wok filled with 1 inch of water. The plate should be about 1 inch smaller in width than the pan to let the steam rise up over the buns, which must sit above the water, not in it.

5. Bring the water to a boil. Invert the dumplings onto the heatproof plate. Place the plate in the steamer or on top of the ring or can in the pan, cover, and steam the buns over medium heat 10 minutes. Serve hot.

Baked Vegetable Dumplings

These are the healthiest of the dim sum. In addition to being wonderful hors d'oeuvres, a few with soup, or grain or rice dishes or with spareribs can add up to a meal.

Yield: 24 dumplings

DOUGH

---

2 teaspoons	active dry yeast
2 cups	bread flour
2 tablespoons	sugar
½ teaspoon	salt
¾ cup	water

FILLING

---

1 teaspoon	vegetable oil
¼ cup	grated carrot
1 teaspoon	minced fresh ginger
1	garlic clove, minced
2	scallions, chopped
1 cup	soy or mung bean sprouts
2 tablespoons	water chestnuts, minced
1 teaspoon	cornstarch
1 tablespoon	soy sauce

1. Add all ingredients for the dough in the order suggested by your bread machine manual and process on the dough cycle according to the manufacturer's directions.
2. Heat the oil in a wok or large frying pan. Add the carrot, ginger, and garlic and stir-fry 30 seconds. Add the scallions, sprouts, and water chestnuts. Stir-fry for 2 minutes. Dissolve the cornstarch in the soy sauce. Add to the wok and cook over high heat, stirring, 1 to 2 minutes longer, until the sauce just coats the vegetables. If extra liquid remains, drain the filling.
3. When the dough cycle ends, remove the dough from the machine and divide it in half. Roll each half between your palms into a 12-inch rope. Cut each rope into 12 equal pieces. Roll or pull each piece into a 3-inch round.
4. Spoon 1 teaspoon of filling into the center of each round. Pull the edges of the dough up and pinch together firmly to enclose the filling and seal. Place the dumplings pinched sides-down 1 inch apart on a lightly greased baking sheet. Lightly cover and let rise in a draftfree place 30 minutes, or until doubled.
5. Meanwhile, preheat the oven to 375 degrees. When the dough has risen, bake the dumplings 10 to 15 minutes, or until golden. Serve with the soy dipping sauce.

Index

218